GROWING TOGETHER

Harold Steindam

GROWING TOGETHER

SERMONS FOR CHILDREN

Illustrated by J. Parker Heck

THE PILGRIM PRESS · NEW YORK

Scripture quotations from the Revised Standard Version of the Bible are copyrighted 1946, 1952 and © 1971, 1973 by the Division of Christian Education of the National Council of the Churches of Christ in the U.S.A., and are used by permission.

The trade name Ivory is used in sermon 33 by permission of The Proctor & Gamble Company.

Library of Congress Cataloging-in-Publication Data

Steindam, Harold, 1950–
    Growing together: sermons for children / Harold Steindam.

    Includes index.
    ISBN 0-8298-0800-0 (pbk.)
    1. Children's sermons.   I. Title
BV4315.S685   1989
252'.53—dc19   88-28718
                                                            CIP

The Pilgrim Press, 132 West 31 Street, New York, N.Y. 10001

Contents

Introduction

THE CHILDREN'S SERMON as a part of weekly worship has become a fairly common feature in American churches over the past ten to twenty years. This has been sufficient time so that people are now beginning to reflect on its appropriateness in worship. To say the least, there are mixed reviews. There are those who are excited and affirmative of children's sermons "because the children are so cute," or "because they help bring more people to church." There are others who are opposed for reasons that sound similar! Some critics even charge that children's sermons may be similar to past presentations of Christmas pageants or other "church spectaculars" in which children were "put on display" and made to say lines they were supposed to memorize but could not understand. In these cases the children were cute—and the adults did come in large numbers—not to hear a message, however, but to see how the children would "perform." Often in these circumstances the greatest responses from the audience would be to the embarrassing moments that would inevitably occur.

Happily, more and more churches are rethinking that approach to Christmas or other pageants, realizing that it is an unfair situation for young children. If there is in my church or others, any similarity to this kind of approach in our children's sermons today then we most certainly must rethink and make great changes in this area, as well.

I am a strong believer in the importance of the children's sermon in the service of worship, but it is with a very different attitude than described above. The reason for including it cannot be that "the children are cute" or that "they bring in more people," but that there is a very real experience of wonder and awareness for both the children and the adults. The children are *not* "on display" and the adults are *not* "an audience." Rather, all are participants in a part of worship that reveals a deeper, more innocent, more real part of ourselves.

*   *   *

I believe there is a very solid basis for the practice of children's sermons, and I believe that basis comes from the Gospels themselves. Our Gospels make it very clear that Jesus took time to be with children, that they wanted to be with him, and that they were at ease with him, and that their parents wanted them to be with him, too. According to John's Gospel (ch. 6:1–10) it was a boy who felt comfortable enough with Jesus to come forward and offer his loaves and fish which Jesus would then use to feed the five thousand. In the Synoptic Gospels (Mark 10:13–16 with parallels in Matthew and Luke) we read that when the disciples tried to prevent parents from bringing their children to him, Jesus became indignant with the disciples. "Let the children come to me," he said, and emphasized that it is in becoming *like a child* that we may enter God's realm.

In Matthew 18:1–5 (with parallels in Mark and Luke) Jesus called a child to come and stand in the midst of the disciples, in an effort to teach them about humility and about entering the realm of God. So, too, we today have much to share and much to learn by calling children to come forward in our midst. The children's sermon can be such an important and positive part of the Christian community's worship experience, as long as it is approached with the kind of care and love that Jesus had as he called children forward and related to them.

*   *   *

I once felt that the most important result of any children's sermon had to be the *lesson* it taught. When I sent the children back to their families after the children's sermon, I hoped every adult would know we had "taught the children something."

However, in reading through the various accounts of Jesus' encounters with children, it one day struck me that nowhere in the Gospel is a single lesson recorded that Jesus taught the children. The Gospel writers go to great lengths to stress how Jesus took time with children, and how they loved to be with him. But there is not mentioned a single lesson he taught them. There are lessons Jesus taught adults, through the presence of children, but not lessons taught directly to the children. I had to think extensively about what this might say to us.

A Christian education professor of mine often said that Jesus played with children and taught adults, while in the church today we have turned this around. So it is that we think there must always be a clear lesson taught whenever we gather children, while for adults a potluck dinner or hayride are considered completely sufficient for a time together!

Clearly for Jesus, the important matter, in spending time with children, was not the lesson but the *relationship.* With Jesus, the children did not learn *facts* about God's love. They learned how it was to *feel* God's love. The children wanted to come to Jesus, not because he taught them verses to memorize, but because they felt his acceptance and understanding. They knew that their worries and wonderings and wishes all mattered to Jesus.

Above all else, the children's sermon must be a time for building relationships with the children. In a week-to-week time together, generally meeting in the very same place, the pastor or other worship leader becomes more and more comfortable with the children; they all *grow together.* The setting is important in that there are adults all around, who are participating by seeing and listening. The love the children feel through the warmth of smiles and other signs of affirmation from these adults is very important. The very fact that the children are called forward, that all the adults present are in agreement that this time is important, sends a great message to the children.

Yet, though it is set in the midst of many, the children's sermon is still a private time for the leader and children. Thus the leader uses vocabulary not for adults, but for children. The leader talks *to* and *with* the children, not to the adults, and never looks out to the adults, but *only* at the children during this time.

A very important beginning to each children's sermon is for the leader to greet each child by first name. This creates an important atmosphere that will greatly affect whatever may follow in the rest of the time together. Names are so important, and over time together they can all be learned and used with frequency. In being called by name a child feels that he or she is known and loved. As we read in Isaiah 43:1, "I have called you by name, you are mine."

Following the greeting of each child, a topic for discussion is introduced. (Yes, there *is* an idea to be shared—and this book is filled with such ideas!) However, the leader always keeps in mind that the relationship is more important than the lesson. As much as possible, the leader asks questions that do not call for correct answers so much as for ideas. The leader is sensitive to concerns that may be on the children's minds, and listens to hear things that may take the experience that day in a different direction than he or she had originally planned. In my use of the story included in "The One Not Handicapped," about the blind college student during a fire in his dormitory, the children had so many questions about being sightless—including questions about braille, guide dogs, and so forth—that it was necessary to take far more time than I usually plan for the children's sermon. During discussion about Abraham Lincoln in "A Leader Who Was Led," mention that Lincoln's presidency was during the Civil War caused one child to speak with great fear about possible war today. Though it deviated from my planned course for the day—and what I present in this book—it was more important to respond to those fears. At the same time, I found that there were ways the lesson I had planned still could relate to those fears, but I had to be sensitive in how that could be done.

A relationship means openness. This is possible when we know that no matter what, God's love is greater than anything we may ever face. Within this confidence we can share these five or seven or however many minutes together, relaxing in a setting that does communicate God's love for the children—and for all present who are also seeking to enter God's realm by becoming like children.

* * *

We *all* grow together in a time in which we are being children who are entering God's realm. Hence we have the title for this book. A leader is not just a teacher but a fellow learner with the children, learning from them as well as teaching them. The leader, children, and surrounding adults are all *growing together.*

There is in the Gospels one more reference about children—about Jesus as a child. In Luke 2:52 the writer affirms the ways that Jesus grew and notes that Jesus grew "in stature." Children are excited by their growing, and many good topics for discussion can be the ways we can see how they are growing in size and ability.

At the same time we are excited about the ways children are growing on the inside in terms of what they are feeling and are now capable of understanding. Like Jesus, they are also growing in wisdom.

* * *

After much reflection on this matter, I have come to believe that we can approach the children's sermon as Jesus showed us in the Gospels. We can create and be part of a setting that leads us to grow in relationship with the children, and to see them not as objects to be viewed, but as fellow members of the realm of God that Jesus wanted us to enter. We can see in them the gifts of humility, excitement, and joy that will enable all of us to grow as Jesus' disciples, and to be part of that realm.

These "lessons" are not ones briefly memorized and then soon forgotten, but ones that last a lifetime. For they become part of our fabric, part of who we are. This happens when we do not just talk about God's love, but together experience it. The greatest benefit that the children's sermon offers is the very opportunity to grow together in such an ongoing relationship of love.

THE SEASON
OF ADVENT

1 · God's Relay Team

SCRIPTURE: *Mark 1:2—"Behold, I send my messenger before thy face, who shall prepare thy way."*
OBJECT: *The Sunday bulletin.*
CONCEPT: *We prepare ourselves to know God and have Christ in our lives through worship and through sharing God's message in our daily lives.*

Good morning! And how are all of you feeling today? . . . Good! I'm glad you are, because we need to be in good shape as we talk about what I want to discuss this morning.

I have here a copy of this morning's bulletin. Many people like to save their Sunday bulletin, so that all through the week they can think about the things we shared in worship. Do you sometimes save yours? . . . Good!

There is one man in our church who does something that I think is extra special with his bulletin each week. His name is Dr. McHugh, and I began to notice that each week he would roll his bulletin up like this and then carry it out in one hand as he left the church.

One day I asked him why he does this, and he said it is to remind him of the time when he was a runner on a relay team. Does anyone here know what a relay race is? What makes something a relay instead of a regular race? . . . Very good, Christy. A relay is a race that involves a team. Usually four runners are on a team, and each one runs a certain distance and then hands a baton—which is about the size of this rolled-up bulletin—to the next person. After all four runners have had a turn and run so far, then the race is over. The whole team together either wins or loses, and teamwork is very important. They all cheer for one another and count on one another, and how smoothly they can hand off the baton to one another and keep it going is very important.

Dr. McHugh says that after worship he always rolls his bulletin like this and thinks about how he is part of God's team, in the same way that we count on one another to take the good news of God's love out to all the people we will see or be with in the coming week.

Think about this. It really is true. Some people think church is over for another week when our service of worship is over. But our real service is just beginning then. We all work together to live as Jesus' followers and be part of that team of Christians throughout the world.

Today we are beginning one of the most important seasons of the church year. We are beginning the season of Advent. For four weeks we will be thinking especially about Christmas and how we can be ready, how we can be prepared, for the coming of Jesus. I think Dr. McHugh's idea is a very good one for us to remember. Taking our bulletins and carrying them like this can remind us of how our service to God just begins with worship each week, and of how we are on a team together, preparing the way for Jesus to be right here with us every day.

Remember, you and I and all of us here are part of God's relay team, as we treat people with love and spread the news of God's love, this day and each day. This is the way we begin to get ourselves ready for the coming of Christmas.

---

2 · Receiving as a Gift

SCRIPTURE: *Luke 7:38—"Weeping, she began to wet [Jesus']*
feet with her tears, and wiped them with the hair of her
head, and kissed his feet, and anointed them with the
ointment."

OBJECT: *Something that has been given to you by someone*
in a special way.

CONCEPT: *When persons feel a desire to be giving, it is*
important to receive their gifts and to understand how
important their giving is.

Today I want to talk to you about something that may be
hard to understand at first. It is somthing very important,
though, and so I hope we can think and talk about it
together.

I want to tell you a story about something that once
happened to my wife, Jenny, and me, and it has to do with
this little pitcher I'm holding. When I was the pastor of a
different church, my wife and I were invited to dinner by a
woman in our congregation—we'll call her Sarah Brown.
Her home was very simple and plain. She did not have
money for "extras" or special things. She cooked a very nice
meal for us, and as we were eating, my wife noticed this
very pretty cream pitcher that was sitting on the table. You
can see how nice it is *(Holds pitcher for everyone to see)*.
Jenny told our hostess how pretty the pitcher was.

"Do you like it?" she asked.

"Yes, I think it is really nice," my wife replied. And do
you know what happened then?

"Well, since you like it so much, I want you to take it as a present from me," our friend said to us.

We replied that we could not accept such a lovely gift from her. But she was so serious and wanted us to have this so much that we changed our minds. We saw how important it was for her to give it to us, and we accepted it graciously.

Do you think this was a good thing for us to do? Or do you think we were not very kind to take something so pretty from a person who did not have very many special things? Do you have any ideas about this? . . . Good, Chad. . . . Good, Robbie. . . . Thank you for all your ideas. We can see that this is a hard question and a hard thing to understand, isn't it?

We decided to take the pitcher because we could see that it was more important to Sarah to give it to us than keep it for herself. Do you know what I mean by that? . . . Have any of you ever been so excited about giving someone a present that you just couldn't wait until he or she opened it? That is a wonderful feeling, isn't it?

Jesus *gave* in many ways to many different people. But he also *accepted* gifts that others wanted to give to him. Jesus knew that it is important to give—and it is also important to receive, so that other people can have the happy feeling of being givers. Jesus knew that when people want to give something really special, they are feeling close to God and want to share God's love.

Well, I said that what we were going to talk about was a little bit hard to understand, and it is. But you have had very good ideas, and I thank you for listening to me and talking with me about this.

Especially as we are coming closer to Christmas, and as we think so much about gifts, it is important to think about what it means to give and to receive gifts. Do you know what? Every time my wife and I see this little pitcher, it makes us think about our friend and we remember how happy it made her to give this pitcher to us. This gift keeps on giving, because it makes us want to be as kind as Sarah, and give more to others, too, and to be as happy as she was when we do so. That is the best meaning for a gift to have— a gift at Christmas or at any other time of the year.

3 · A Gift We Often Forget

SCRIPTURE: *Ecclesiastes 3:1—"For everything there is a season, and a time for every matter under heaven."*
OBJECT: *A large piece of cardboard with 1,400 X's on it.*
CONCEPT: *One of God's gifts to us is the time that we have.*

We're getting closer and closer to Christmas. Yes, it's less than two weeks away now, isn't it? What are some of the things we think about in this time of the year? . . . Decorations . . . presents . . . the baby Jesus . . . yes, those are for sure all on our minds these days.

As we think about presents, we know that God has given us the greatest present of all, and that is Jesus. But God gives us so many other presents, too. I have something here to help us think about one of the most important gifts of all.

This looks pretty funny, doesn't it? *(Holds up cardboard with X's on it.)* Yes, it shows lots and lots of X's. Do you know how many X's are on this piece of cardboard? There are one thousand four hundred and forty. I have put that many here because this is how many minutes there are in every single day. Did you know that? Well, there are!

Tell me, what are some things you can do in one minute? Can you think of something? . . . Yes, commercials on television sometimes last a minute, so you can watch one of them. Corey says he can tie his shoes in a minute! That's good. Setting up the checkerboard for a game does take about one minute, too, doesn't it, Casey?

There are some things we must do every day. We must take time to sleep and time to eat and time to go to school or do other important things. Almost every day, though, there is some time left when we can do whatever we choose to do.

All the time that we have comes from God. It is a present from God to us. And we can sometimes choose to make a present for someone else out of our time. In one minute you can help carry your dishes from the table after dinner. Or in one minute you can tell your mom or dad or brother or sister how much you are glad for him or glad for her. Or in one minute you can start to draw a picture or make a card or think up a story for someone. I have heard about families who try to do things like this for each other during the Advent season, just to make Christmas an even happier time of the year, and many of these nice things can be done in just one minute.

There are many, many things we can do with the minutes we have. We can turn many of them into presents for others, and when we do that we are making a present for God, who has first freely given us all the time that is ours.

I hope you will remember this piece of cardboard I have today. Or maybe you can make one thousand four hundred and forty X's on a page sometime yourself, to help you think about how much time God gives us every single day.

When we think about presents, remember, God gives us so many presents—including all the time that we have. And we can turn some of our time into presents for others by choosing to do things that are thoughtful and kind.

4 · The Light Continues

SCRIPTURE: *John 1:5—"The light shines in the darkness, and the darkness has not overcome it."*
OBJECTS: *Birthday candles that relight themselves.*
CONCEPT: *The light of Jesus Christ in the world cannot be put out.*

We are getting so close to Christmas. Yes, just a few more days! On our Advent wreath all the candles are lit now except the Christmas Eve candle. We know that we are very close!

Christmas is Jesus' birthday, and since this is the Sunday that is closest to his birthday, I thought we could celebrate together this morning. What are some things people do at birthday parties? . . . Play games . . . have presents . . . eat cake and ice cream. . . . Yes, those are all wonderful, happy things! What do we put on the cake at a birthday party? . . . Of course, Andrea, we put candles on it. Usually, we put one candle for every year of age of the person whose birthday we are celebrating. Today I am going to use just these four candles, though, because that is how many candles are lit on our Advent wreath this morning. I'll light them from the candles here . . . and let's sing to Jesus. . . . Now, some of you may blow out the candles. . . . Hey, what is happening? I thought you did a good job of blowing them out, but they are burning again. OK, Joshua and Jordan, why don't you try? . . . Oh, dear, they are back again!

What, Heather? You think these are trick candles? . . . Oh, you know about these candles already? Yes, you are right. These are special candles because Jesus' birthday is a special day!

The Bible tells us that Jesus is like a light that comes into a dark place, and no matter what happens, the light does not go out.

Sometimes scary things can happen. Sometimes very sad things may happen to us. But no matter what happens to us, and no matter what happens anywhere in our world, we know that God is with us through Jesus, and God will help us to be safe and to know what is right and always to have hope for good to come.

Birthdays are happy times. Jesus' birthday is an especially happy time for everyone! That is why these special candles are so important, because they help us think about the ways Jesus' birth is so special. I hope you will remember these candles. And most of all I hope you will remember God's message to us—that since Jesus was born, his light has been in the world with us, and *nothing* can ever put that light out.

CHRISTMASTIDE

5 · Batteries Included

SCRIPTURE: *Luke 2:20—"And the shepherds returned, glorifying and praising God."*

OBJECT: *Some kind of toy that requires batteries.*

CONCEPT: *The time after Christmas is not a time of being "let down" but a time for new energy because of Jesus' birth.*

Did all of you have a happy Christmas day? . . . Good, I am so glad you did. Did any of you receive a special present for Christmas? . . . Those are all such wonderful things. I have here a present that was given to me. It is a toy car that looks very nice, but I am afraid it doesn't do anything special. According to what is on the box it came in, it is supposed to zoom across the room if I push this little button. But look, when I press it, nothing happens. Oh, well, it still is nice to look at and set on the shelf. . . . What, Sara? What do you say it needs? . . . It needs a battery? Why would it need that? . . . I see. A battery gives the car energy. A battery will make it go and be what it is supposed to be.

Well, let's see. Let's put a battery into it and see if that makes any difference. . . . Ryan, push that button and . . . wow! Look at that! You were right! A battery makes all the difference. Now it looks good and it is fun, too!

Sometimes, after Christmas, people feel a little bit sad. Did you ever feel that way? We think about how Christmas is over now and won't come again for another whole year, and we are very sad as we put away all the decorations and stop singing our favorite Christmas songs.

But do you know what? If we do that, then we are being just like this toy when it doesn't have a battery. We don't have the energy and the excitement inside us that Christmas truly brings, because Jesus *really has* been born and is with us now.

Sometimes things *look* so nice—just as this little car looks nice. But what is more important is what we feel *inside*. Jesus has been born, so it isn't just that Christmas looks pretty, but it really is how we feel and what we do. Knowing that Jesus has been born, we don't feel sad that Christmas is over. Instead, we feel so happy because Christmas has come, and we know Jesus will be with us through the whole new year. We have energy—we have batteries!

I hope all of us will be like a toy with the battery put in. I hope we will have all the energy and excitement to tell everyone that Jesus has been born and is with us. That is good news—the greatest news. It is so great and we are so happy that we celebrate with parties and presents. That is why we have given and received little cars and other special gifts.

Now let's know that the celebration isn't over—it has only begun! Our batteries are in, and we are energetic, because Jesus has been born and is with us.

6 · So Far, So Good

SCRIPTURE: *Isaiah 41:10—"Fear not, for I am with you, be not dismayed, for I am your God."*

OBJECT: *A lantern or a flashlight.*

CONCEPT: *There is much about the future we cannot know, but we do know that God is with us today and as we go into the future.*

New Year's Day is coming this week and I've been hearing many people talking about what may happen during the coming year. Especially, I've been reading and hearing stories about *predictions*. Do you know what a prediction is? . . . Yes, Curtis, a prediction means telling what may happen someday far in the future.

Some people wonder or worry about what may happen next month or next year. And so they listen carefully when they hear predictions being made about what could come about.

I heard a story one time about a boy who was afraid of the dark. He lived on a farm, and at night he was afraid to walk by himself from his house to the barn because it was very dark on the way. His mother wanted him to know he would be safe, though, and that he did not need to be afraid. So this is what she did.

One night as they stood at the back door of their house, she lit a lantern—like this one—and it spread light in a circle all around him. Then she told him that he could walk to the barn. "But I still can't see the barn," the boy said.

"No, you can't," his mother replied, "but you know what direction the barn is in, don't you."

"Yes," he said, "it's over that way."

"Well," his mother told him, "just carry your lantern and keep walking out to the edge of your light in the direction of the barn."

So that is what the boy did, and what do you think happened? . . . Very good, Michael. As he went, the light went with him. And so he kept going and going, until finally he could see the barn and was safely there.

Have any of you ever noticed, riding in your car at night, how the car's lights shine just a short distance out in front? But the light keeps going, just enough in front of the car, so the people inside can go safely as far as they want. Just as in the story of the boy who walked to the barn, the light goes with us, just far enough ahead for us to be safe.

This story helps us to think about how God is with us. We don't know everything that will happen in the future. We can't see way ahead to know all the things that will happen in this new year ahead. But we do know that God is with us *right now.* God has always been with us, whatever we have done or wherever we have been, and God promises to be with us each day, no matter what happens. God's light travels with us, just as the light from the boy's lantern did. When we walk in the direction that we know is right, God's light keeps going just as far and just as fast as we do.

Sometimes it can be fun to make predictions about what might happen in the future, or to listen to other people's ideas. But the most important thing is to know that no matter what is ahead, God is going to continue to be with us. God's promise to send Jesus to us has been kept. And God's promise to be with us this day and each day will always be kept. We are not afraid, because God's light is always surrounding us.

EPIPHANY
AND THE
SEASON
FOLLOWING

7 · *It's Up to Us*

SCRIPTURE: *2 Corinthians 5:17—"If anyone is in Christ, he [or she] is a new creation."*
OBJECT: *Pads of clean paper.*
CONCEPT: *From God we receive—and through Christ we appreciate—the gift of each new day.*

Does everybody remember Christmas? Yes, it was nearly two weeks ago now, wasn't it? Do you remember the things you were given as gifts? . . . You say that some of them are broken, or don't work already? That happens sometimes, doesn't it? But even though some things may not last long, the meaning of Christmas still does last. It goes on and on within us.

Many of you mentioned special gifts that you received and that you are continuing to enjoy. I am going to show you one of the gifts I received that is a special favorite of mine. Look what I have here. . . . Yes, Anne, it is a big pack of paper. And to be exact, it is a pack of twelve legal-sized tablets. Jenny gave these to me because she knows I like them so much and use them for many different things.

Let's get one out and look at it. You can see that nothing is written or drawn on any of the pages. It's up to me, as I look at each new page, to decide what to do with it.

Tell me some things that I could do with this first, clean page of paper. . . . I could draw a nice picture or write a kind letter or write down ideas for church school class. Those are very good ideas for things I could do. . . . Or I could just scribble on the page and waste it. It really is up to me, isn't it? to decide if I will use it for good and helpful things or not.

Today is the first Sunday of this new year. Who can tell me how any months there will be this year? . . . Right, twelve—just like my twelve pads of paper! And how many weeks will there be? . . .Fifty-two—yes, the same as last year. Kelly! How many days? . . . You got it, Thad! How many hours? . . . Hmmm, I guess we need a calculator for that, but we know there will be many.

Every new day comes to us as a gift from God. Every day is like a new sheet of paper on a new pad, and we are free to decide if we will just be wasteful with it or if we will use it for good things.

Christmas was just a couple of weeks ago, and Jesus is with us now as we are starting this new year. No matter what may be ahead for us this year, we know that God will be with us through Jesus. And we know that all the time that God gives us every day of this new year will be a gift that we can appreciate and use for good things that will show God's love in our lives.

8 · Work While You Whistle

SCRIPTURE: *Philippians 3:14—"I press on toward the goal."*

OBJECT: *Just yourself—or anything that can represent something you have been working to learn or do.*

CONCEPT: *Things that we want to learn to do often take much time and commitment.*

Today I am going to tell you something about myself that makes me very sad. Part of me doesn't even want to tell you, because I am a little bit embarrassed by it. What I have decided to tell you is that I have never learned how to whistle. It is true. I wish very much that I knew how. I think there are many times when knowing how to whistle would come in very handy or be very helpful. I could get someone's attention very quickly, or I could whistle songs to keep me feeling happy while I am working or out walking.

But I cannot whistle. When I was about seven or eight, and many of my friends were trying to learn how to whistle, I was trying to learn, too. But I didn't try very long. It seemed too hard, and I was frustrated that I wasn't learning to do it faster, so I just quit. I'm going to try right now, and show you how well I can do it. . . . Well, you see that I can whistle a little, but not very much. What about you? Are any of you learning to whistle? May I hear you? . . . Oh, my, Joshua and Heather and Jillian—you are all doing very well!

Tell me, what is your secret? How can I learn, too? . . . I see . . . put my lips like this and blow. I'm still not getting it. What else must I do? . . . Practice? Is that what you said, Lindsay? Do you mean that I need to try and try, and not give up even if I don't learn how right away? I think you are right. I think that is the real secret.

Some things just take time. Learning to play some games well or learning to read or learning to play a musical instrument—all these things take much time and much practice.

We are still in January. It is a new year. Many people make resolutions at the beginning of the year. These are promises to do something different in the new year. But then it seems to be harder and harder to keep learning or doing the new thing. We really must stick with it, every day and every day, if we are going to learn something new. This is true with all the kinds of things we mentioned earlier—things like games and musical instruments—but it is most true of all with learning to be good Christian persons. We can always be learning more and more in following Jesus.

I hope you will remember my whistling. I cannot do it very well because I never stuck with it. But you are right in what you said. I need to practice and practice. I need to work at whistling, so that I can one day be whistling at work!

I hope you will remember that there are many things we can learn to do better and better, but we need to stick with them and not give up.

We are glad that God has made us so that, by practicing over a period of time, we can learn to do so many different things.

---

9 · God with Us

SCRIPTURE: *John 1:48—"Nathanael said to [Jesus], 'How do you know me?'"*

OBJECT: *A tape recorder.*

CONCEPT: *God is not distant. Not only is God with us through words but truly with us as a living, caring being.*

Do any of you have a favorite story—one that you like to hear again and again? Maybe it is one that you like to hear when you are getting ready to go to bed. . . . Yes, Jennifer, I like that one, too. . . . I don't know that story, Erin, but it sounds nice, too. It must be, if it is your favorite!

I know a little girl who had a favorite story. Every night Susan wanted her father to read that story to her at bedtime. Finally, her father got an idea. He made a tape recording of the story and showed Susan how to run the tape recorder so she could listen to it whenever she wanted.

This seemed to work for a while, but then one night Susan brought the book to her father and asked him to read it to her. "Now, dear," her father said, "you know how to turn on the story on the tape recorder and hear it there, don't you?" And she answered, "Yes, I know how to hear the story on the tape recorder, but I can't sit on its lap!"

When her father heard that, he realized it wasn't just the story that was important to Susan. It was being together and sharing his love with his daughter that was even more important than the story he read. Now Susan listens to the tape recorder sometimes, but usually her father holds her on his lap while he reads it to her.

This makes me think about how God is with us and how God loves us. We are glad that we have the Bible and all its stories about God and how God loves us. But God did not just give us the Bible and then go away. God is right here with us, loving us, so close to us. We are held by God and can be as close as when sitting on our father's lap.

God is with us through Jesus, who lived among other people just as we do, and who showed most of all how loving God is and how God knows each of us so completely.

God is also with us through the special persons in our lives—fathers and mothers, grandparents, teachers, and good friends. When people know us and care about us, they are helping us to feel God's love. Through Jesus, through special people in our lives, through the Bible, and through so many of the happy things we see and do, we know that God is not far away from us but right here with us. It is just as though we get to sit on God's lap while we hear our favorite story being read with love to us!

10 · Keeping an Eye on Groundhogs

SCRIPTURE: *Matthew 16:2—"When it is evening, you say, 'It will be fair weather; for the sky is red.'"*

OBJECT: *None required, although pictures or items from nature may be used.*

CONCEPT: *We can learn about weather—and so much more—from the world of nature and from within ourselves.*

Tomorrow is going to be a holiday, and it is one of my favorites! Do you know what day it will be? . . . Of course! It will be Groundhog Day! Tell me about groundhogs. What are they? . . . Yes, Eddie, they are animals that dig in burrows and make homes underground. What is another name for groundhogs? . . . Yes, Karen, they are also called woodchucks, and there is a tongue twister about how much wood a woodchuck could chuck, isn't there? . . . What, Erika? You say that your father doesn't like groundhogs? . . . I am not surprised. Many people don't like them, because they can get under houses or other buildings and do damage when they dig their burrows. However, when they live in the wild and let us live where we live, they are just fine.

Now, tell me about Groundhog Day. How does it work? . . . I see. . . . That's right. On February 2 the groundhog comes out of the burrow where he's been living during the winter. If he sees his shadow, then that scares him, and he hides again for six more weeks of winter. But if the groundhog doesn't see his shadow, then that means spring is just around the corner.

Do you think this is really true? Do groundhogs really look for their shadows on a certain day, and does winter really depend on that? . . . No, it doesn't really, does it? That is just for fun. It is something for us to talk about and think about in the middle of winter.

But do you know that some animals really do tell us about winter? People who study the weather have learned that how some animals build their homes for winter tells how cold it will be. Some caterpillars have more "wool" growing on them when the winter is going to be extra cold. We don't know how these animals know this, but somehow they do. Somehow, God takes care of them in this way.

God takes care of us, too, by helping us to use our eyes and our minds to notice and to prepare. We can look at the sky and the clouds and know when we should get ready for rain or snow or some other kinds of weather.

Even more than that, God helps us to see other things with our eyes and think about them in our minds. These things help us to become more prepared to be Jesus' followers in whatever we do each day.

We don't believe in groundhogs the way that is pretended on Groundhog Day. But we do believe that all around us God is giving us signs in nature that help us to learn and know what to do. And we believe in ourselves, that we can learn from what God wants us to see, and be caring Christians who are growing each day in God's love.

11 · Keeping (Warm in) the Faith

SCRIPTURE: *2 Corinthians 5:7—"For we walk by faith."*
OBJECT: *A child's blanket sleeper.*
CONCEPT: *No matter where we are, or where we go, our faith strengthens us and guides us.*

Can you tell me what this is that I am taking out of this bag? *(Pulls blanket sleeper out of bag.)* . . . Yes, I think all of you know what it is. It is a kind of pajama outfit for children. At our house we usually call these "bear" pajamas, because our favorite brand has a bear on the front. But Kristen is right. The "official" name for this is "blanket sleeper."

Why would this be the name for it? Can you tell me? . . . Yes, David, it is a sleeper—which is another name for pajamas—and it is like a blanket, because it is extra warm. Here, you can feel how warm and furry the material is. . . . Yes, many of you already know, because you wear them, too, don't you?

Since we have had children at our house, we always make sure they wear a blanket sleeper to bed during cold weather. We put the blanket sleeper right over their pajamas. The reason that parents like to use these for their children is that they stay on all night, keeping the children warm. If we use a regular blanket, it comes off when the children roll around in their beds and move about while they are sleeping, and they get cold. But the blanket sleeper stays with them—from the neck right down to the toes—no matter how much they move or even if they get up from their beds.

In the same way, we know that God is with us no matter where we go. Some people used to believe that God was only with them when they were in their church. But that is not so. God is with us if we are at church or at school or at home or outside playing. No matter where we go, God stays with us, helping us, just as this blanket sleeper stays with us when we put it on.

It is important always to remember how God is with us and how we have faith in God to help us, whether we are happy or sad or lonely or afraid. No matter what, no matter where, we can be sure that God is with us.

Whenever you see a blanket sleeper and you think of how it does its job of sticking with you and helping you feel warm and good, I hope you will think of how we know that God is always with us—loving and caring for us wherever we are.

12 · A Leader Who Was Led

SCRIPTURE: *1 Samuel 16:13—"Then Samuel took the horn of oil, and anointed [David] in the midst of his brothers; and the Spirit of the Lord came mightily upon David."*

OBJECT: *A picture of Abraham Lincoln, or any object relating to one of the stories about him.*

CONCEPT: *Lincoln is considered by many people to have been our greatest president. He accomplished so much good because he always relied on God and on scripture.*

This coming week will be the birthday of someone very important in American history. Do you know whose birthday will be on February 12? . . . That is right, Nathan—Abraham Lincoln. He was born in 1809, and he was our nation's sixteenth president.

Many people think Abraham Lincoln was our greatest president ever, and one of the finest persons ever. I want us to talk about him this morning. Maybe you could tell me some of the things you have learned about him in school or at home.

(Here the children may be encouraged to tell some of the things they have learned about Lincoln. Or one of the many short but excellent books about him for children may be read. How much time is spent and how much detail on any area is pursued depends very much on the leader of the group and on what parameters she or he wishes to set.)

I want to share a couple of things with you that I think are important in telling what kind of person Abraham Lincoln was. One is a story about him while he was president. One day Lincoln was sitting in his office, polishing his boots. One of his advisors came into the president's office and was surprised to see Lincoln doing this. The adviser said, "Mr. President! Important people don't polish their own boots!"

And President Lincoln said, "Oh, really? Whose boots do they polish?" President Lincoln turned the question into a joke, because he didn't think that he was more important than other people or that he should have servants do everything for him just because he was president.

The most important thing I want to tell you is that Abraham Lincoln always depended on God. He learned the same Bible stories you are learning in church school and at home, and he always tried to follow those lessons in the way he lived and in the way he led our country.

When Lincoln was elected president and left his hometown to go to Washington, the last thing he said in a speech to his hometown friends was this: "Without God's help, we cannot succeed, but with God's help, we cannot fail." In his speeches and in his decisions, Abraham Lincoln often used quotations from the Bible to help him. Through all the things he did in his life, and through all the hard things he had to do while he was president and the Civil War was going on, he was always led by the lessons of our Bible and our Christian faith.

This is what I hope you will remember about Abraham Lincoln—that he did many good things during some very hard times and that he was able to do them because he depended on God. Remember, we can depend on God to lead us and to help us to know what to do and to have courage to do it, every day, just as Abraham Lincoln did.

THE SEASON
OF LENT

13 · Rewriting the Recipe

SCRIPTURE: *Matthew 13:33—"The [realm] of God is like leaven which a woman took and hid in three measures of flour."*

OBJECT: *A pad and marker with which to write down what the children say.*

CONCEPT: *Our lives are made up of many "ingredients." Our faith is the ingredient that blends everything together in just the right way.*

Lately I have been feeling very hungry for cookies, and I think I would like to try making some myself. Can you guess what my favorite kind of cookie is? . . . Yes! Chocolate chip is right! How many of you like chocolate chip best? . . . It looks as though most of you do!

Well, I need you to help me know what to mix together and what to do in order to make two dozen chocolate chip cookies. That would be twentyfour—and I think that should hold me for a day or two!

OK, what is the first thing I need? . . . Ah, yes, Kershel, a bowl—a big bowl! OK, I'm writing down "Take a big bowl." Now what do I put into the bowl? . . . Chocolate chips? Great! How many do I need? . . . A bag? What size bag? . . . A *big* bag? Excellent! What else do I need? . . . You are right, Kesha, I need flour. Four cups, you say? . . . What's that, Tahdi? . . . Yes, I need to make dough out of this to make it into cookies, don't I?

What other ingredients do I need? . . . Eggs . . . three

or four of those . . . and sugar . . . OK, lots of sugar . . . oil and vanilla and a little bit of salt, and . . . what, Frederick? . . . Oh, yes, we'll need lots of milk for later when we are ready to eat our cookies, won't we?

I think there is one ingredient still missing, something that will make what we bake be light and crunchy and really be a cookie. Do you know what I mean? . . . Yes, Shawn, something like yeast. Yes, baking soda or baking powder—which has a kind of yeast in it—needs to go in.

Baking powder doesn't taste very good by itself, does it? But if we put just a little bit into the bowl and mix it in, what a difference it makes! It makes the dough rise while it is baking, and makes it taste really good.

There are many different ingredients that go together and make up our lives. All of you are part of a family and a home. Most of you go to school. You all have neighbors or special friends who play with you. Many of you spend time learning to play musical instruments or some kinds of sports. Those are all good and important things. But do you know what? There is one more ingredient that is just like the baking powder. It is our faith in God. Our faith tells us how God wants us to live our lives in order to learn and grow and use our talents. Our faith blends through all of our lives and helps everything to work together and be better and happier.

Today we are beginning the very special season of Lent. During this season we think especially about the different parts—or "ingredients"—of our lives, and of how our faith in God can bring the best to all of those parts, how it can bring all those parts together in the best ways.

Well, I think we are just about finished with our cookie recipe. Now we need to bake it for how long? . . . An hour and fifteen minutes—at 100 degrees? *That* should be interesting! Maybe we'll publish this recipe in our church's newsletter for people who are hoping to try it!

The next time you eat a cookie, I hope you will think about all the ingredients that have to be mixed together to make it good. And I hope you will remember the important job the baking powder does. It is just like the job that our faith does. It is the ingredient that brings the best out of all the other ingredients of our lives.

33

14 · Licking Problems

SCRIPTURE: *Matthew 25:35—"For I was hungry and you gave me food, I was thirsty and you gave me drink, I was a stranger and you welcomed me."*
OBJECT: *A picture of an ice-cream cone.*
CONCEPT: *There are many needs that cannot wait but must be responded to as we learn of them.*

Spring will be here in a few weeks now, and it's nice to think about the warmer weather that's coming! The ice-cream parlor across the street has opened again, and they have let me borrow this picture of an ice-cream cone. . . . It looks really good, doesn't it?

Does anybody here like ice cream? You do? What flavor do you like best? . . . Chocolate . . . Strawberry . . . Mint chip . . . That's my favorite, too. More votes for chocolate, and a couple for vanilla, too. . . . What, Dionna? . . . You don't care what flavor, just so there's lots? I think we know what you mean!

Think with me for a minute about the weather and what it will be like in a couple of months. It will be really hot, won't it? On a hot, sunny day, suppose you get an ice-cream cone, but you don't want to eat it right away. . . .

Suppose you just want to look at it and think about how nice it looks. What will happen if you do this? . . . Yes, that is easy to figure out, isn't it, Sara? The ice cream will start melting very fast. It will drip all over your hand and onto the ground. When you have ice cream on a hot day, you know you have to keep on licking it or else it will melt and your chance to enjoy it will be lost.

There are some things that we can save, some things that can wait until we are ready for them. But thinking about the ice-cream cone reminds us that there are also some things that cannot wait. For example, when someone needs our help, we cannot wait. We need to do whatever we can to help that person right away.

When someone is hurt on the playground, you know to get help for her right away, don't you? There are other kinds of hurts that need attention right away, too. There may be a time when you know of someone who is afraid or lonely and needs to talk to a friend. You can reach out to that person and be that friend right when he needs you.

Today our church is having a special offering called One Great Hour of Sharing. Part of this money will be kept in a special fund—ready to help right away—when there is an earthquake or flood or some other kind of emergency any-where. When we give money to this offering, we are helping to meet problems at the moment they happen.

From now on, when you have an ice-cream cone or see a picture of one, I hope it will remind you of what we have talked about today. I hope you will remember that just as ice cream melts if we wait too long to eat it, we also can't wait about some other things. I hope it will remind you that there are some things that we need to do to be helpful to others right at the moment of their need or it may be too late to be of help.

15 · So Tiny—But So Big

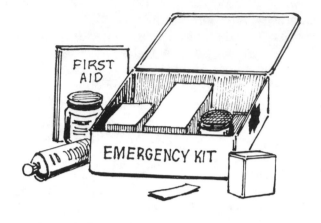

SCRIPTURE: *Psalm 19:12—"Clear thou me from hidden faults."*

OBJECT: *A very tiny sliver of wood.*

CONCEPT: *Some habits or faults that we think are small may be more harmful to us than we think.*

Last summer our family went to Yellowstone Park. While we were there, we wanted most of all to see Old Faithful. Do any of you know what Old Faithful is? . . . Yes, it is a geyser. That means it is hot water coming out of the ground that shoots high into the air. Do you know how big Old Faithful is? . . . Yes, it is very big. It shoots water more than one hundred feet into the air. That is higher than our church.

We went to see Old Faithful, but do you know what? At first I couldn't see it, and I couldn't see it because of something that is so little you may not even notice it, even though I am holding it in front of you right now.

Look at this. Can you see it? It is a very tiny sliver of wood. Have any of you ever gotten a sliver of wood into your hand? . . . Or knee? . . . Yes, Violet, that is easy to do, too—and it hurts very much, doesn't it?

While we were walking out to see Old Faithful, my hand brushed against a piece of wood, and a sliver of it went into my hand. It was such a little thing, but it hurt so much! It hurt so much that it made tears come into my eyes, and I couldn't see Old Faithful. We had to go back to our car for our first aid kit to get a needle to remove the sliver. Then I was able to go back and see Old Faithful and really enjoy watching it.

Sometimes we begin to get a bad habit. Maybe we tell little lies or we do little things that aren't very kind to someone. We may think our action is such a little thing that it really does not matter. "That can't do any harm to me," we say.

But we can be wrong about this. Just like a little sliver of wood, a little habit really can hurt us. It can get in our way and keep us from being able to see all the things and do all the things and be all the things that will make us the happiest and best persons we can be. Anything that we know is wrong can get between us and God, and that is very, very sad.

The season of Lent is a time when many people make the decision to try to change things about themselves. They may give up something or try to do something extra each day that will help them to become better persons. Perhaps you know of some habit that would be good for you to change in your life, and this special season would be a good time for you to begin that change.

After we got our first aid kit and took the sliver out, how much better I felt! And how much I enjoyed looking at all the beautiful things at Yellowstone Park!

The next time you have a sliver or know of someone who does, think about how important it is to get it out right away. Remember also how important it is to remove any little thing that might come between you and God. How much happier you will feel when you do!

16 · Not Missing the Important

SCRIPTURE: *Luke 8:45–46—"Peter said, 'Master, the multi-tudes surround you and press upon you!' But Jesus said, 'Some one touched me.'"*

OBJECT: *An apple with the stem attached.*

CONCEPT: *Sometimes the things we overlook or do not think too much about are the most important. The same can be true of the persons in our lives.*

I have here one of my favorite snack foods. It is a good, healthy kind of snack. . . . Yes, Nicholas, it is an apple. When our children are hungry, we often give them an apple, because it is a natural food, full of vitamins and good for our whole bodies, including our teeth.

We have only *one* apple here, don't we? Yet, each apple has a number of different parts to it. I wonder if you could tell me which of the parts of the apple is the most impor-tant. . . . Think about it. Think about the inside and the outside. What is most important? . . . OK, Clinton says the meat of the apple is most important. That juicy, inside part is what tastes the best of all, isn't it? OK, Karen, you say the skin of the apple is the most important. And why is that? . . . Yes, it is what protects the inside so it will taste so good, isn't it? Also, the skin has many of the vitamins we need.

Do you have any other ideas about what is important? . . . Ah, yes, Ashley, the seeds, inside the core. That is also very true, because they can help us grow more apple trees in the future.

Well, we've named different important parts of the apple. But what about *this* part? No one named the stem. Does it matter much? . . . No, we might just as well throw it away.

But first, let's ask what job the stem had. What did it do? . . . That's right, Megan, the apple hung from that on the tree. And what happened *through* the stem? . . . All the nutrients that would make the apple grow and create all the important parts we have named came through the stem. It is what made it possible for the whole apple to grow.

Sometimes we don't notice things that are really important, because they aren't very showy or big. But like the stem of the apple, they may turn out to do some of the most important jobs of all.

Some people are very quiet and we may not notice them at first, but then we find out later that they are some of the nicest and most caring people anywhere. Here in our church there are some people whose names we don't hear mentioned so much, but they are so very important, working behind the scenes and doing really important jobs.

Maybe in your neighborhood or at your school or even in your family there are persons who are sometimes not noticed very much. I hope you will think about what may be special about those persons, and think about how they might be best friends. Think about what you can do to show you can see those special gifts they have.

From now on, whenever you eat an apple, I hope the stem will remind you of what we have talked about today. The stem is what made it possible for the whole apple to grow. I hope that noticing the apple's stem will help you to notice other things that are important—and especially other people—when they aren't the ones who get our immediate attention.

17 · *Every Place Is Holy*

SCRIPTURE: *Matthew 6:28—"Consider the lilies of the field."*

OBJECT: *Something that came from the Holy Land.*

CONCEPT: *Jesus has taught us that all places are holy, because God is in every place.*

You can see that I have a tiny container here. It is clear, and in it is some water. This water came from a place far away from here. It is called Holy Water, because this came from the Holy Land.

Do you know what it means when someone says "the Holy Land"? . . . Right, Shawn, it means a holy place. Do you know *what* holy place? . . . You have a pretty good idea, don't you, Vanessa? The Holy Land is the land where Jesus lived. It is far, far away from here, clear over on the other side of the world. Many people want to travel there, because they want to see the places where Jesus once lived.

A friend of mine who went on a trip to the Holy Land

brought this water back to me so that I would have some-thing from that special place. That was really nice for him to give me this present, and it is nice when people get to go there and see those places.

But do you know what? Even though it is wonderful to visit the land where Jesus lived, it really is not necessary to be in the land where Jesus lived to be in holy land. I want to talk more with you about what I mean by this.

Jesus did not do or talk about things that can be seen only in the place where he lived. Instead, whenever Jesus talked to people or taught them, he always talked about things that can be found almost anywhere. Jesus talked about birds, about flowers, about seeds—about things that are here where we live, just as they were where he lived.

So if we think about the land where Jesus lived as holy land, then this place where we live is a holy land, too. We have birds and flowers and seeds and all the other things Jesus talked about in his teachings. And if God cares for these everyday things—everywhere—how much more God cares for human beings throughout the world. So Jesus talked about trust in God and about caring for our land and the people around us.

I am glad that I have this little vial of water from the Holy Land, the land where Jesus lived. I am also glad that we have pictures of the places where Jesus walked and talked to use in our church school classes. But I am even more glad that Jesus taught us that God is everywhere and that our land is holy, too.

I hope we will remember this, and always be looking at the birds and flowers and other everyday things around us, and think about what they can teach us of how God is with us and always loving us.

I hope we will think about how the place where we live—right here in our town—is a holy land, because God is here.

18 · Seeing God in the Beauty

SCRIPTURE: *2 Chronicles 5:1—"Thus all the work that Solomon did for the house of the Lord was finished."*
OBJECTS: *Cathedral cookies* (see recipe on page 44).
CONCEPT: *We do not have to worship in a beautiful place in order to see and know God. Yet we want to make our place of worship a beautiful place, as it reminds us of the greatness of God.*

It is so good to be with you in this place of worship. I believe that our church is a very beautiful place. . . . Do you think so too, Meredith? I am glad you do. What are some of the things that you think make this a pretty place for us to gather for worship? . . . Yes, I like that, too . . . Very good . . . Ah, yes, Matt, I agree. The stained-glass windows make our church especially pretty.

Since the time of King Solomon, way back in the Old Testament, people have wanted to make the places where they worship God as beautiful as they can. Hundreds of years after King Solomon, but still hundreds of years before our time, one of the things created that is especially beautiful for churches was stained glass.

When stained-glass windows were first made, they had pictures of stories about Jesus. It was before the time of the printing press, so people did not have books. They could look at the windows, though, and learn the stories of Jesus. Today many churches have stained glass, and sometimes the windows have pictures of stories from the Bible. But we especially admire them because they are so beautiful.

Do you know that God is with us wherever we are? . . . Yes . . . you all know that very well. We do not *have* to be in a beautiful place for God to be with us and for us to worship God. But people *want* their place of worship to be beautiful, because it reminds them of the beauty of God's love and the glorious things that God has made. That is what stained-glass windows help us do. They help us think about the beauty and glory of God's great love.

We usually wear nice clothes and want to be clean and look our best when we come to worship. We do not *have* to do that, because we know that God is with us no matter how we look. But as much as we can, we want to look our best and be at our best as we think about God's wonderful love for us.

Ever since Bible times, people have wanted to have beautiful places for their worship. We are glad for this beautiful place, and glad that our church inspires us to be at our best and do our best to be God's people and help others. We are very glad for the stained-glass windows that we have that tell us stories and help us think about the wonder and beauty of God.

I have a special treat for you this morning. I have a cookie for each one of you. . . . Yes, they do look good, don't they, Ben? They are called cathedral cookies, because they look like stained-glass windows. They are pretty, and they taste good! When you eat yours, I hope you will remember what we talked about this morning—how we are so happy to have our special windows in our church. We do not *have* to have them to worship God, but we are glad we do. They remind us of God's glorious love. Beautiful things can inspire us to think more about God and to want to do more to serve God.

CATHEDRAL COOKIES

1 12 oz.	pkg. chocolate baking bits (or chocolate chips)
¼ lb.	margarine
1 c.	coarsely chopped nuts
1 10 oz.	pkg. multicolored mini-marshmallows
1 ½ c.	grated coconut

Melt chocolate bits and margarine in a double boiler. When they are completely melted, set aside to cool to lukewarm temperature (it should not melt the marshmallows when they are added).

When the mixture is cool, add nuts.

Empty package of mini-marshmallows into a large mixing bowl. Pour cooled chocolate and nut mixture into the bowl and mix together. Divide into three portions. Shape into rolls.

Divide coconut into three portions and spread on three sheets of wax paper. Coat each roll with coconut.

Refrigerate. With a wet knife, slice in ½-inch slices.

HOLY WEEK

19 · In Partnership with God

SCRIPTURE: *John 6:35—"Jesus said to [the people], 'I am the bread of life.'"*

OBJECTS: *A loaf of bread, a bag of flour, and some stalks of wheat.*

CONCEPT: *In communion we eat bread, which symbolizes Christ, who unites us with God, just as the bread itself shows this unity.*

We have talked at different times about what communion means. Today I want us to talk more about communion. To do that, I have brought one of the two elements used in communion. I have here a loaf of bread. Can you tell me what the bread means in the communion service? . . . Yes, Colleen, it means Jesus' body, and it reminds us that Jesus' body was broken for us, as he died for us.

In order to make bread, what do we need? What is the main ingredient? . . . Right, Suzanne, it is flour. There are different kinds of flour, and each kind can help make a different type of bread.

Now, let's go back one more step. What comes before the flour? What is flour made from? . . . Yes, indeed. Flour comes from wheat. I have some stalks of wheat right here, and you can see that they have little kernels in them. When they are crushed and ground, they turn into a powder which is flour.

Every loaf of bread comes about as a result of a partnership between God and people. I want you to think with me about this idea of a loaf of bread coming from partnership between God and people. What are some of the things God must do to help make a loaf of bread come about? . . . Yes, God makes the wheat grow. God sends sunshine and rain—not to mention the great miracle that makes growth possible, so this wheat will grow in the field.

But then people must take over and do their part. What are the things that are up to people to do, in order to have bread? . . . Yes, they must gather the wheat . . . and make it into flour . . . and mix it and bake it and make the bread. That is very good. God must do one part, and people must do another, and that is how we come to have each loaf of bread.

Jesus chose bread for us to use in remembrance of him, because Jesus shows a partnership between God and people. Jesus was divine—that means Jesus was part of God. And Jesus was also human—that means he was part of people. Jesus did not sin, but still gave his life for us. Then God brought Jesus back to life, and that brings us together in a new way with God.

Again, the first part is done by God, sending Jesus to us. Then we are able to do our part, and that is to accept that Jesus is our Savior.

Every time you eat bread—and I know that is often, because bread is such an everyday food—I hope you will think about this and will remember Jesus and what God has made possible for us through him. Remember that every loaf of bread shows how we are in a partnership with God. Remember how Jesus makes the greatest partnership of all possible, as we are brought so close to God through Jesus.

This is a very important part of understanding the meaning of communion, and I thank you so very much for talking and thinking about this important subject with me today.

20 · New Life from Old

SCRIPTURE: *Matthew 16:21—"From that time Jesus began to show his disciples that he must go to Jerusalem and suffer . . . and on the third day be raised."*
OBJECT: *A book showing pictures of a dead tree and what becomes of it.*
CONCEPT: *In God's plan, even a dead tree has many purposes in bringing life to plants and animals. In this we see signs of God's care for us—care that goes beyond and is greater than death.*

At the library there are books on all subjects, and we can learn so many things by getting books at our library. One of my favorite topics is God's world of nature, and there are many books that can teach us more about that subject. I have a book to show you this morning that tells us what happens in a forest and how different plants and animals live there.

One section of this book is especially interesting to me. It shows what becomes of a tree after it has died in a forest. I always thought that once a tree died, it was not good for anything, except to be cut down and taken out of the way. . . . Is that what you thought, too, Adam? Yes, I thought that was so.

But let's look at these pictures together. . . . Here we can see how some birds still make nests in a dead tree, especially because now that its wood is getting softer, different kinds of insects are living in it, and they make food for the birds. . . . Here we see how toadstools and other fungus plants are growing on the dead tree now, and that brings still other kinds of animals to it. Once in a while, a dead tree will become hollowed out, and that makes a nice home for larger animals like skunks, or maybe even a mountain lion. . . . What, Lindsay? You say there are lions in our town? . . . Hmmm . . . the only ones I know of meet for lunch at the restaurant every Monday! . . . Finally, as the years go by, we see that the dead tree is breaking down into new, rich soil, and that is helping new trees and other plants to grow in its place and to keep the forest alive and healthy.

It is so amazing to me to think about what wonderful plans God has made to take care of all the plants and animals of the forest. In God's plan, even a dead tree is part of bringing about new life, helping the plants and animals that God has made and loves.

This week we are talking about the saddest thing that ever could have happened—that Jesus was put to death on a cross. Yet we call this day "Good Friday," because God turned this into a *good* day by bringing Jesus back to life on Easter. Again, we see that God's plan is greater than anything, even greater than death. This was true for Jesus, and through Jesus we know it is true for each of us, as we are God's children.

I hope you will go to the library soon and perhaps look at books about nature. Maybe you will even get a book like this, with pictures that show what happens to a dead tree. Perhaps you can tell a friend what we have learned about trees and about God's plan for the forest.

Then remember how God was with Jesus and is with you. God is greater than anything and everything in our world. God can turn all things into good and has a plan and a purpose in all things.

EASTERTIDE

21 · Where Are We Looking?

SCRIPTURE: *Luke 24:5—"Why do you seek the living among the dead?"*

OBJECT: *An Easter egg.*

CONCEPT: *Because of the resurrection, Jesus is with us in all parts of our living.*

I am going to tell you something this morning that I thought I would never admit to anyone. Here is what it is. When I was a child, every Easter the colored eggs would be hidden in our house, and my sister and I would hunt for them and see who could find more. My sister was three years younger than I was—so when I was eight she was only five, and when I was nine she was only six, and so on. But do you know what?—and here is the hard part for me to admit. Even though she was younger than I was, every year she still would beat me! She would always find more eggs than I did! You can imagine that I wondered why she always found more eggs than I did. I'll bet you would wonder what you were doing wrong if Erin always found more than you did, wouldn't you, Brent? . . . Well, so did I!

Finally, one year I asked her. I said, "Shirley, how do

you always find so many?" And here is what she said to me.

"Harold," she said, "if you are going to be good at this, you have to *think like an egg!* You have to ask where good places would be if you were an egg and wanted to hide, and then look there!"

Tell me, do you like to go on Easter-egg hunts? . . . Yes, I think we all do. We had a fun hunt here at our church this morning, didn't we? It is really fun to look and look, and then so exciting when we spot one! One of the reasons we have egg hunts on Easter is that it reminds us of how happy and excited people were when they first discovered that Jesus had come back to life. Easter is the most exciting and happy day of the year for Christians, and hunting and finding eggs is one way we *do* something that acts out our happiness and excitement.

People on Easter morning went to find Jesus. But they looked in the wrong place. They looked in a place for persons who had died. But then they were told that they would not find Jesus in a place for the dead, because Jesus was alive! Then they knew they were looking in the wrong place, so they went to the places where they had been living, and they found Jesus in all those places.

I said that Easter is our most happy day—but actually every day can be happy and exciting for us now, because Jesus has come back to life! Jesus is alive and with us in all the places where we live. Jesus is with us when we are at church. Jesus is with us when we are at home. Jesus is with us when we are on the school bus or in our family car. In all the places where we live, Jesus is right there with us. Jesus is with us when we are with other people and when we are alone.

I hope that when you are looking for eggs and you find one and are excited, it will remind you of how people felt on the first Easter. And I hope you will remember how every day can be a happy and exciting day because of God's love for us through Jesus.

Let's remember to keep looking in the right places for Jesus. Remember, Jesus is with us in all the places where we are living. I hope you will have a very happy Easter, and then remember that *every* day is a happy day for us *because* of Easter.

---

22 · Eyes to See

SCRIPTURE: *Luke 24:32—"Did not our hearts burn within us while he talked to us on the road?"*
OBJECT: *Pieces of paper cut into the shapes of the drawing on this page, and a piece of cardboard.*
CONCEPT: *For those with faith, Jesus, who has risen, can be seen in many places.*

What I am going to do with you today is a little bit like a puzzle. I am going to take all these funny-looking shapes and stick them onto this cardboard. As I go along, I want you to tell me if you know what I am making.

First, I'll put this piece here . . . and now this piece. It looks funny so far, doesn't it? Now I am putting another piece in place . . . and one more. Nobody knows what this is yet? OK, here is the last piece.

Oh, Tammy knows! Yes, it says "Jesus." Can the rest of you see it now? Here is a plaque that Tammy's family gave to me, with the same thing on it. I think that is why she recognized it first, don't you? Can you see the word, "Jesus" now? . . . What if I hold my hands to make a line above and below it? . . . Ah . . . now more of you can see it. Even when I take my hands away, you can still see it, can't you? At first this looks as though it is just a funny picture of shapes. But once we see the name of Jesus, then we can see it every time, so easily.

Last week we were all so happy as we celebrated Easter. That is wonderful, but we know that the happy celebration is not over—it only *began* last week. Now we know that Jesus is not dead, but is risen and is with us.

After the crucifixion, Jesus' followers were very sad. They thought they would not see Jesus again. But God brought Jesus back. And while two followers were on the road to Emmaus, Jesus came near and went with them. At first, in their sadness, they did not recognize Jesus. Later, as Jesus broke bread with them, their eyes were opened and they recognized the risen Christ, just as we see the name "Jesus" on this plaque if we really look.

Because we know that Jesus is risen and with us, we can see him in so many places. We can see Jesus when we are with loving people like our family members or teachers or friends. We can see Jesus when we watch someone being kind to someone else. We can see Jesus when we pray alone or when we come together for worship. We can see Jesus when we follow his teachings and love one another.

The picture on this plaque is becoming special to more and more people, so we see it more often in different places these days. I hope that when you see one of these and you are able to see the name of Jesus right away, it will remind you of all the ways we can see Jesus in our lives. We see Jesus because we believe in Jesus as Savior. We know that we can see Jesus, who rose from death and is always part of our lives.

23 · *Our Silent Partner*

SCRIPTURE: *1 Corinthians 3:6—"I planted, Apollos watered, but God gave the growth."*
OBJECTS: *A hoe, a rake, or other gardening utensils.*
CONCEPT: *Though it is not always immediately or easily seen, God is always working with us.*

As you can see by this hoe, I have something in particular on my mind today. This is one of my favorite times of the year, because it is the time that we really get busy in our gardens.

Do any of you like to work in a garden? . . . Some of you do. What do you like to do, Kyle? Do you like to hoe? . . . Good, because that is a really important job. It keeps the ground nice and soft as the young plants are growing. Do any of you like to help with the planting? . . . Corey and Kara do. Do you get everything planted in straight rows? . . . Sometimes? Good! Pulling weeds out by hand is important, too, isn't it? . . . No, Christy, that isn't my favorite part, either. But it is very necessary if we want our garden to produce healthy vegetables.

Later in the summer, if we have done all these things, then we'll probably have many good things in our garden.

What do you like to eat from the garden? . . . Carrots . . . pumpkins . . . good. What about spinach? . . . hmmm . . . not much enthusiasm about that! My favorite food from the garden is potatoes. When they are finished growing, I like to dig into the ground for the potatoes, and it's just like discovering treasure as we see how many there are!

I remember a story about a girl named Barbie. She found an abandoned area of land that had really become a mess. She was told that she could have this land for a garden, so she really went to work. She picked out the litter and the rocks. Then she dug up the ground and planted seeds. After that she hoed it and watered it and cared for the plants. Everything grew and grew, and the garden looked beautiful.

One day a man walked past and said to Barbie, "That certainly is a beautiful garden that you and God have there." And do you know what Barbie said?

She said, "Yes, but you should have seen it when God had it alone!"

It sounds funny that the man thought Barbie and God were partners in the garden, but he really was right. What did God do as one partner in the garden? . . . That is right. God gave the sun and the rain—and the seeds and the miracle of growth. God made the seeds become plants and the plants finally become full grown.

It was possible for seeds to grow into plants in that place before Barbie came along. But when she got to work and did her part, then what was possible could come to be. God does not make gardens grow alone, and neither do people. But when God and people work together, then the miracle of growth can take place in our gardens.

This is true in many other situations also. In our homes, in church school or weekday school, God is there, acting as our partner. Sometimes, if we don't stop and think about it, we don't realize all that God is doing in these places as our partner. But God is always there—in other places as surely as in the garden.

I hope we will always know how much God is our partner, and produce the best things in our gardens and the best things possible in ourselves because of that partnership.

---

24 · *Playing Catch with God*

SCRIPTURE: *Job 38:4—"Where were you when I laid the foundation of the earth?"*

OBJECTS: *A baseball and glove.*

CONCEPT: *We are blessed to enjoy the world that God has created for us.*

Now that we are in one of my favorite seasons of the year—the baseball season—I have brought my baseball glove and a ball with me this morning.

I want to tell you a story about a girl who took her ball and glove and started to go into the backyard to play. Her father saw Chris going out by herself and asked, "Are you going to play by yourself?"

Chris answered, "God is going to play catch with me."

Wondering what Chris was thinking, her father asked, "How can God play catch with you?"

"It's easy," Chris explained. "I throw the ball up into the air and God throws it back down to me!"

What do you think about that story? Do you think God was really playing catch with Chris? . . . No, God wasn't playing catch with her in the ways we usually think of. We all know that if we throw something up into the air, it just comes back down to us automatically.

But let's think about this story some more. What is it that *makes* the ball come back down? . . . Of course, Karin, it is the law of gravity. But why is there a law of gravity? Who made gravity, anyway? . . . Yes, God made all the laws of science and nature that there are. God made the law of gravity, so that when we throw a ball up, it will come back down to us. So in a way, Chris really was right, wasn't she? In a way, God was playing catch with her.

God created our world in all the ways that make playing baseball or any other game possible. There is the law of gravity, and there are also the laws about how objects are moved when they hit into each other or how they are affected by the air. We do not know how all these laws of science and nature came to be. We were not there when God made the world just this way.

But even though we were not there and do not know everything that God did to make the world the way it is, still we can enjoy it. We can depend on balls coming back to us when we throw them up. We can depend on so many things always being just so, every time they happen. That is why we are able to play and work and live as we do.

The next time you go out to play baseball or any other game, I hope you will remember the story of the little girl who was playing catch with God. I hope you will know that whatever you are playing or doing, God really is there with you, because God made our world, with all the good and dependable things there are about it.

25 · We Make a Difference

SCRIPTURE: *Proverbs 15:6—"In the house of the righteous there is much treasure."*
OBJECTS: *A glass jar of water, some food coloring, and some white wildflowers.*
CONCEPT: *Because of God's love, each of us makes a difference in the world, especially in the ways we influence others.*

Sometimes I feel discouraged. Do you ever feel discouraged? I think we all do sometimes. Every now and then, I find myself thinking that this world is so big, and I am so small. I hear about sad things that are happening, and I wish I could make them stop—but I know that I can't. When I think like that, I feel very discouraged. I start to think that it doesn't matter very much whether I try to do my best or not.

But do you know what? The Bible teaches us that it really *does matter* that we do our best. It matters because of *who we are*. The Bible teaches us that we do make a difference by how we act and how we try to care about one

another. The Bible says that inside each one of us is treasure. It is sort of like buried treasure. And when we try to
do our best, God is with us and is helping that buried
treasure to be uncovered.

I want to show you something. Here I have a big jar of
water, and here I have a tiny bottle of food coloring. The
water jar is big and the coloring bottle is little, and it
doesn't seem that a small amount of coloring could make a
difference in a large quantity of water. But . . . look. I am
going to put just one drop of the coloring into the jar of
water. . . . There it goes. Look, it is slowly, slowly spreading. . . . Now look. The whole jar of water is changing to a
reddish color, just from that one drop going into it. That is
what the Bible wants to teach us—that even if we feel
small, we can still make a difference because of God's love.
Whenever we are doing our best to care about the persons
around us, and whenever we are doing our best in any
activity, then we are like a drop of color that is spreading,
spreading, farther and farther, in ways that will make a
difference to the people around us and a difference in what
kind of world there is.

I have something else here. It is Queen Anne's lace.
You have all seen these flowers, haven't you? They grow
wild in many places. If we pick some of these wildflowers
and put them in water that has food coloring it it, do you
know what happens? . . . That's right, Nicole. Slowly, the
flower begins to change to that color.

You may try this, with your parents' help, at home. You
will find that the change doesn't happen all at once. It takes
time. But, slowly, the flowers absorb and take on the color
of the water they are in.

We can be just like that coloring in the water. Our
treasure can come out and we can slowly make a difference
in the people around us. I hope you will ask your parents to
help you try some of these things at home. Maybe you could
make a bouquet of all different colors of flowers.

Remember, it takes time. Remember, over time we
really do make a difference, because God is with us, helping
us to bring out the treasure that is inside us.

---

26 · A Wonderful, Playful God

SCRIPTURE: *Psalm 77:14—"Thou art the God who workest wonders."*

OBJECTS: *A handful of maple seeds.*

CONCEPT: *Not only does our world have beautiful things but also things that show what God is like.*

Good morning—and it is a good morning! This is one of my favorite times of the year. Spring is such a beautiful season, as so many things are happening in our world. It is the season in which we have celebrated and now continue to celebrate Jesus' resurrection, as we see signs of new life in so many places all around us.

In my hand I have some things that are landing all around us these days. These are maple seeds. But I know there is a much better name that children have for these seeds. What do you call them? . . . Of course, Johnny, you call them "helicopters"! And why do you call them that? . . . Yes, because they fly through the air, looking just like helicopters. They are made in just such a way, with just such a shape, that when they fall from the tree, they do not fall straight down, and they don't float along as some other seeds do. Instead, they are exactly such a shape that when they fall from the tree, they will spin and spin and float along in a wonderful and fun way.

Why is it important for these seeds to float away from their tree? . . . That is right. It is so that new trees will grow in other places. If the seeds just came straight down and landed below their tree, they could not grow there. But if they can float to other places, they may be able to start growing as new trees there.

So that is the reason the seeds have to float away some distance—but I have still been wondering more about just why it is that they would be shaped in this particular way. Who do you think has made them to be in this exact shape? . . . Joey is right. God has. God has made all the things that are growing to be the shapes that they are.

But I am trying to figure out why God would make these seeds in this way. After all, God could have made them some other way and still had them float farther from their tree. Do you know what I think? I think that one important thing for us to know is that God likes to have fun—and likes us to have fun, too! That is the best reason I can find why God has shaped these seeds in this way.

I am going to throw some of these seeds up in the air so we can see what they do. . . . I can't get them up as high as they are in the trees, but . . . oh, look! Some of them really are going into a *spin*, and they do look like helicopters!

And listen to you! All of you are laughing and becoming excited and happy while the seeds are coming down. God truly did make a special gift for all of us to see and have from watching these seeds in their flight.

When you think about God and what God is like, you may think about how God is so big and so powerful. And that is OK, because that is true. But at the same time, I hope you will think about things like these "helicopters," and remember that one of the most important things about God is that God loves us and wants our world to be a beautiful, happy place for all of us to live.

---

27 · *Bearing Fruit*

SCRIPTURE: *1 Timothy 6:20—"O Timothy, guard what has been entrusted to you."*

OBJECTS: *An apple, a sharp knife, and a plate.*

CONCEPT: *As we grow, we learn more about ourselves—and God knows all about our growing and loves us as we grow to be all we can be.*

I am glad to have all of you with me this morning, and I am especially glad you all look so alert, because I have two questions that I want to ask you.

Are you ready? Here's the first question: How many seeds do you think there are in this apple? Think about that. I am sure you have all eaten apples right down to the core and seen the seeds inside. How many do you think there are? . . . Missy says four . . . Kim thinks seven . . . and Kristen says eight . . . I'm also hearing votes for six and five. Those are all good guesses. Well, there is one sure way to find out, and that is to cut the apple apart and see.

OK . . . I am doing that. Let's see . . . there are two in this section, and two more in this one. There are two more here, and one in this last one. So, the answer for this apple is seven. I think it was Kim who guessed that number, and it was right in this case. All your guesses were good, though, because it could have been any one of those numbers.

What, Ginger? . . . You want to eat some! OK, let me cut these into more pieces and pass them around.

While you are each taking a piece, I want to ask my second question. Do you remember that I said I would ask a second question? The second question is, How many apples are there in this seed?

Do you think that is a funny question? Scott says there aren't any apples inside this seed, and in a way he is right. But think more about it . . . OK, Steven says ten! . . . Marcy says one hundred, and Michelle says a thousand. Why do you say a number that big, Michelle? . . . Yes, that is right. If this seed is planted in the ground and grows into a tree, then it can make hundreds and even thousands of apples. No one knows for sure how many.

Some things we can know for sure. We can look inside an apple and find out how many seeds are in it. But we can never know how many apples might come from one seed. Only God can know that.

There are some things we know about ourselves. All of you have been growing and learning to do different things. You all know about some of the things you can do and how you have learned them. But you are all going to keep growing and learning and doing more things. Do any of you know *all* the things you will do in your lives? . . . No, of course not. But God knows. God has given you all the abilities and possibilities that you have, and God is going to be with you as you keep on learning and growing.

Each one of us is like a seed, and we don't know all the things that are going to come from us. But God is with us, loving us and helping us as we go along and grow along, learning and doing all the things that are possible for us.

THE SEASON
OF PENTECOST

28 · All to the Good

SCRIPTURE: *Philippians 1:22—"Yet which I shall choose I cannot tell."*
OBJECT: *Pictures of various flavors of ice cream.*
CONCEPT: *God often gives us many choices for good in our lives.*

I have heard something that is hard to believe. I have heard that Friday was your last day of school and that you now have vacation from school for the whole summer! Is that true? . . . It is! And you all seem pretty happy about it, too, don't you?

This is going to give you lots of extra time. Tell me, what are some of the things you plan to do with your time this summer? . . . Danielle says she is going to go to Florida. And Eric says he is going to Niagara Falls. So some of you will be going on vacation trips somewhere. That is great!

What are some other things you can do, right here at home? . . . Play with friends . . . go swimming . . . go to the library . . . play baseball. Good—those all are good things. The activities you have named are all good choices. They are some of the many, many good choices you could have named.

As we think about choices, I want to show you a picture that our dairy store across the street let me borrow. Yes, yum! These pictures remind us of some of the flavors of ice cream they have there. Tell me something: when you go to the dairy store or to some other place that has many different flavors of ice cream, how do you choose which one you will get? What method do you use? . . . Neil says he always chooses chocolate chip! That must be your favorite flavor, and you know you can't go wrong with it. What are some other ideas? . . . Chris chooses the one that sounds best that day. That is a good idea, too. Erika? . . . You start at one end of the freezer and work your way across! I like that! So every time you go, you get to try something new. That is another great idea.

You have many different ideas, and they are all good. It is nice to have so many choices of good things when we are at our favorite place.

Today is a happy day. As you begin your summer vacation time, I hope you will think about all the good things that God gives us to be able to do. There are so many good choices, so many good things we can do with our time and our energy this summer.

I have a present for each of you. In celebration of all you learned at school this year and in celebration that vacation has now begun for you, we have a gift coupon for each of you. Your coupon is good for a free ice-cream cone at the dairy store across the street. . . . You are very welcome. Just promise me one thing—that when you go in and look at all those flavors of ice cream, and choose which you will have, it will remind you of what we have talked about today. I hope it will remind you of what a loving God we have and of how God gives us so many good choices of what we can do and what we can learn each new day.

29 · *Pretty Smart!*

SCRIPTURE: *Titus 3:14—"And let our people learn to apply themselves to good deeds."*

OBJECTS: *A variety of simple objects, about ten to fifteen in total.*

CONCEPT: *God has made us with minds that can learn, remember, and do so much good.*

Today is graduation Sunday, and we just honored all the students from our church who are graduating this year from high school. Did you see all of them when they were up here? They are pretty big, aren't they? And they surely are smart, too, to be graduating from high school.

Some of you have big brothers or sisters who will be graduating before long, but all of you have many more years to go, don't you? Let's see . . . Rosa, how many years will it be until you graduate? Ten years—that is a long time. . . . Elizabeth says there are seven more years for her. That is not quite as long, but still a long time . . . Yes, that is more years than many of you are old right now! What about

Jessica? She will not be in kindergarten for two more years, so there will be fourteen or maybe fifteen more years for her!

For all of you, it will be a long time until you graduate from high school. But do you know what I think? I think you all have good minds and are pretty smart right now, even though you have many more years until you graduate from high school.

Let's do something together that uses our minds. In this bag I have twelve different things. I am going to set them out in front of you, and then put them back in the bag and see if you can remember all of them. OK? Here we go. . . . OK, they are all out, and you know what they are. . . . Now, let's put them back.

Now that all twelve things are back in the bag, let's see if you can remember what they were. . . . As you say one, I will take it out of the bag. Steven says a ruler . . . and here it is. Yes, yes, . . . a toothbrush and a pair of scissors . . . right . . . one at a time—a pair of scissors, a candle—here it is . . . a shoe . . . yes, a pencil . . . very good, a Cleveland Indians cap.

We are getting close—four to go . . . a pillow . . . three more. Great, Robyn, a calendar . . . a pack of seeds. One to go! The last one is always the hardest. Think . . . think . . . Susan says a paper clip! And here it is, the smallest item of all!

You got them! You remembered all twelve! And how could you do that? . . . That is right: you did it because you really are pretty smart. You did it because you have minds that can remember. And we know who gave you your minds so you can think and learn and remember. God did! God, who loves you so very much.

Many of you are in school now, and others of you will begin someday. In school and at home, in church and with friends, you are always learning more and more.

I hope all of you will be blessed in all of your learning. God wants you to use the many abilities that you have been blessed to have. I hope you will find many ways to use your learning for good, for being helpful and kind to other people. That is just what God wants you to do, too!

---

30 · Deeply Rooted

SCRIPTURE: *Psalm 71:3—"For thou art my rock and my fortress."*
OBJECT: *A dandelion or other weed with a very long root.*
CONCEPT: *When we have faith in God, we are able to be strong even when we face difficulties.*

Do any of you help to work in a garden? . . . Do you, Robert? Perhaps you have a family garden and you help your parents or brothers and sisters there. What kinds of jobs are there in a garden? . . . Yes, planting and watering and weeding. Weeding especially is a big job in the garden.

Have you ever tried to pull dandelions out of your garden or yard? . . . You have? Tell me about dandelions, Marcus. What are some things you know about them? . . . In the springtime they get a yellow flower, don't they? And then that flower turns into white, fluffy seeds that blow everywhere. Children like to play games with the yellow flowers and with the white seeds. I remember that . . . and you say that you do these things, too!

Well, the leaves and the flowers and the seeds that we see are all very important. But there is something else even more important about dandelions that we don't see from just looking at them—and that is their roots. I have a dandelion here that I carefully dug and pulled out this morning. I was careful to get as much of its root as I could . . . and look! I didn't quite get it all, but look how big, how long it is! Why, it is longer than the dandelion that we can see above the ground!

The main reason that there are so many dandelions, and that they keep growing even when someone tries to pull them out, is that they have such deep, strong roots. It is what we *can't* see by just looking at them that makes them so strong.

Do you know what? The very same thing is true about us. What is not seen at first—what is not easy to see on the *outside* of us—is really the most important part of us. The most important part of us is our *faith* in God. That is our greatest strength, and it is deep inside us. It is our root. It is what gives us life and helps us to keep going even if sad things or hard things happen.

We know that God is with us and that God loves us and will guide us no matter what may happen. Knowing that with all our hearts gives us the strength we need when something sad happens. It also helps us to know what is right to do when we have to decide about something that is hard for us.

When you work in the garden, or whenever you see a dandelion, I hope you will notice the parts of it that you can see. Then remember that the part that makes it so healthy and so strong is the part you can't see—and that is the root. And remember that what is most important about you and what gives you your greatest strength is also a part that cannot be seen from the outside. It is your faith in God. That is your root and your greatest strength.

73

31 · Part of a Bigger Story

SCRIPTURE: *2 Timothy 1:5—" . . . a faith that dwelt first in your grandmother Lois and your mother Eunice and now, I am sure, dwells in you."*
OBJECTS: *Seeds or a small tree seedling.*
CONCEPT: *The story of God's love has been passed on to us, and we pass it on to others, knowing we have a part in that story.*

I want you to look at this little plant that I have with me this morning. It is actually the beginning of a kind of tree—a pear tree. If we planted this tiny plant right now, what would happen to it? . . . Yes, Bobby, it would eventually become a full-grown tree. How long do you think that would take? . . . Yes, a long time—probably ten or even fifteen years would go by before it would be full grown. That is how long it will take many of you to be finished growing—at least in some ways—isn't it? That is a long time to wait—a long time until this tree will be giving us pears as a fully grown fruit tree.

I remember a day when I was taking a walk and I met a man. This man was quite old, and he was planting little fruit trees just like this. I thought and thought and wondered and wondered about what he was doing. And I realized that he will probably not be alive when those trees will be fully grown and giving fruit.

74

I asked the man why he was doing this, since he probably won't get to have any of the pears that will grow from these trees. What do you think this man said in answer to my question? Why do you think he was planting these trees? . . . That is a good thought, and so is your idea, Jimmy. Let me tell you what the man said to me. He said that all his life he has enjoyed eating pears and peaches and cherries and all sorts of other fruits that have come from trees that he did not plant. Instead, other people a long time ago planted those trees. And this man says that, thanks to others, he has had all of these things to enjoy. And so, he says, he just wants to say "thank you" by planting trees that someone else will be able to enjoy.

I think that this is a very caring idea, and a very kind thing for him to do. It makes me think about our special church school service today. We are ending our year of church school and getting ready for the new school year that will be coming by celebrating Christian Education Sunday in our church.

For hundreds of years people have been telling others about Jesus and telling others the stories of God's love. These things are here for us when we are growing up, and then we can pass them on to others. This is a little bit like the man and the fruit trees he is planting, because the stories of God's love—especially God's love in Jesus—are bigger than we are and will live longer than any of us.

The stories of God's love make up a story that is bigger than any of us, and yet each of us is still a big part of that story. The story is given to us. It is there, free for us, and we are blessed to receive it. Then we can be like the man who is planting trees. We can pass it on to others as a way of saying "thank you"—and as we do so, we become even more a part of the story. This is what our church school teachers are doing and why we are celebrating their work today. It is something each one of you can do, too, by using the opportunities you have to tell others or show others about God's love.

When we receive the stories about God's love, and when we pass them on to others, we are being a part of that story which is bigger than any of us, yet a part of each of us.

32 · *It Makes Sense!*

Maria Age 6 Maria Age 16

SCRIPTURE: *Proverbs 19:20—". . . that you may gain wisdom for the future."*

OBJECTS: *The children themselves.*

CONCEPT: *God plans for us to learn and grow, slowly and surely, in so many ways.*

Do you know what? I've been noticing that just about every week one of you is having a birthday. At least it seems someone is always talking about a birthday that is coming up! I wonder if that is true today. Is anybody here having a birthday very soon? . . . Yes, Maria, the first week in July? That is soon! And what about you, Reginald? . . . October 15? Yes, that is pretty soon, too!

I think Maria's will be the soonest birthday, though, so I want to ask her some questions. How old are you now? . . . You are seven. How old will you be when you have your birthday? . . . You will be eight! Now that is very interesting to me. After someone is seven, she always turns eight next, doesn't she?

Well, I have been thinking about this lately, and I believe I have come up with a better idea. I think that instead of going in a certain order for our birthdays, we should get to be whatever different age each year we would like to be. Instead of turning eight next week, maybe Maria could turn sixteen! Then some other year she could come back to being eight. Wouldn't that be more interesting and more fun? We could all just jump around to being whatever age sounded the most fun for that year!

Hmmm. Some of you are smiling as though you like my idea. But quite a few of you are shaking your heads. Why is that? . . . You don't think my idea would work. . . . You think it's important to be each age in the right order! . . . Matt has said something that sounds important—and even his brother, Pete, agrees! He says that if Maria decided to be sixteen this year, instead of eight, it might be dangerous if she tried to start driving a car. She wouldn't have had time to get big enough or ready enough to drive a car or to do some of the other things that people are able to do at sixteen.

There are good reasons why we have our birthdays in a certain order, aren't there? Each year in school you are learning new things, things that you are ready to learn because of what you learned in the last grade. When you are five, you are ready for five-year-old things because of what you learned when you were four. And when you are starting the sixth grade, you are ready for it because of what you learned in the fifth grade. This is true no matter what age you are or what age you are becoming.

God really has a wise plan in the way that each one of us is made and each one of us is growing. I hope you will think about some of the things you have learned to do in this year of being the age you are now. For each one of you, I'll bet there are many things you have learned. Then think about all the new things you will be able to learn and do in the next year because of the ways you are learning and growing right now.

And I hope you will remember how much God loves you and how wonderfully you are made. As you grow and grow, it all makes sense—because of God's wonderful plan!

33 · Turned to an Advantage

SCRIPTURE: *Judges 20:16—"Among all these were seven hundred . . . who were left-handed."*

OBJECT: *A bar of Ivory soap.*

CONCEPT: *What makes us different from others can be an important help to us.*

What I have here I'll bet all of you have used at some time—at least I hope you have! . . . Yes, it is a bar of Ivory soap. There is something about this kind of soap that makes it different from any other kind. Do you know what that "something" is? . . . Exactly, Aaron—it floats! That makes it extra handy in the bathtub, doesn't it? It stays on top of the water and doesn't get lost in all the tub toys so easily.

I have learned something about what happened when Ivory soap was first made that is very interesting to me. The first batch of Ivory was made somewhat by accident.

Too much air was trapped inside the first batch, and so the people at the company that made it were surprised, and many of them were very worried because it floated.

Some of them thought that people would not want to buy it because it was different. If it floated, it might not seem as strong or efficient as other brands that could be bought. What, they wondered, should their company do?

But there was one person there who had a very different idea. "Let's not try to hide this, and let's not be embarrassed about it," this person said. "Instead, let's *tell the world* about it! Let's tell about how it is so pure that it floats, and about the advantages of our new product!"

And so they did. And Ivory has become one of the most popular of all soaps in the world. Instead of thinking that what made their product different was a disadvantage, they thought again and saw how it could be an advantage.

This is such an important lesson for all of us. There are things about each one of us that make us different from others. Maybe we hit a ball in a different way. . . . What, Kimberly? Do you bat in a different way than your friends? . . . They made fun of you sometimes, but then you hit a home run that way? Good for you! Maybe we have a different favorite color than anyone else we know, or maybe our voice sounds very different from anyone else's. Sometimes we may feel funny if we think differently from others or do things in different ways. Maybe we even want to hide the differences, the way some of the people at the soap company wanted to hide their difference at first.

But I hope we can remember the lesson that the Ivory soap people learned. Let's remember that what may at first seem like a disadvantage can be turned around and be good for us. What makes us different is what helps make us who we are. If we explore what makes us different and special, God will help us to discover more and more about ourselves, and we will be able to do more.

I hope that whenever you use Ivory soap you will remember the story about it. Remember that floating makes it different, and that is good. Then think about the things that make you different and that can be so important and so good for you.

34 · Sunny Showers

SCRIPTURE: *John 16:24—"Ask, and you will receive, that your joy may be full."*

OBJECT: *A small umbrella.*

CONCEPT: *We must not only pray but believe in God as we do so, living in ways that show our faith.*

I want to tell you a story this morning. I am going to try to tell it to you just as I remember it.

Many years ago I was the pastor of a church that was out in the country, located in the midst of corn and wheat fields. As a matter of fact, nearly every family in that church lived on a farm. One of the summers that I was there, we had sunny weather almost every day. It was nice to have all that great weather, except that it got to be too much of the same thing. Day after day, and then week after week, went by without rain. The fields were getting drier and drier, and everyone was becoming very worried about what would happen if it did not rain soon.

We talked about this at some of our church meetings, and we talked about how much we all believed in prayer. We decided that the next Sunday we would have a special prayer service to ask for the rain we needed so much for the crops. We sent out church letters and advertised in the local newspaper that we would be doing this.

Sunday came, and it was another beautiful, sunny day. Many, many people attended the special service that day. I remember especially a boy named Dennis. When he came into the church, he had one of these *(holds up small umbrella)*, and he said, "I thought that if we were going to be praying for rain, I'd better bring my umbrella!"

Tell me something. Don't you think Dennis was really silly to do that? After all, there wasn't a cloud in the sky that day. Why would he have needed to have an umbrella? . . . You think he wasn't so silly, Chris? Why not? . . . Very good. What do you think, Tim? . . . Your ideas are very good, too.

Yes, it is true that it didn't seem that it would rain that day, but Dennis showed how serious he was about his prayers and how much he believed prayer would make a difference, and that is why he brought an umbrella. . . . Yes, Anne, your mother is right. We *do* need to be careful what we pray for! We need to be ready for God's answers when we pray.

We believe in God and we know that we can pray to God. Jesus told us that God wants to answer our prayers and give us the things that we truly need. A very important part of our believing in prayer is to *act* in ways that show we believe that God will answer our prayers.

If we pray to make up with someone and be friends again, then after we pray, we must act in ways that show we want to be friends and believe we will be again. Doing that will probably even be part of how God makes our prayers answered.

God loves us and wants good things for us. I hope we will always remember this. I hope the story of the boy who brought his umbrella on a sunny day will help us remember what it means to live in ways that show we believe that God will answer our prayers.

---

35 · Let's Face It!

SCRIPTURE: *Psalm 94:9—". . . who planted the ear, . . . who formed the eye."*
OBJECT: *The children themselves.*
CONCEPT: *We have been made with great, loving care by our God.*

As I look around at you, I am so pleased. You all are so special to me, and I want you to know that you all *look* very special, too. You all are just the way God wants you to be!

As I look at you, I am reminded of some of the very special care that God put into *how* you are made. In looking at just your faces, I am reminded of many special ways that God cares for you.

Let's look at Rachel. What are these on the sides of her head? . . . Yes, they are ears! And what do they do? . . . You are right again! Notice that there is not one ear, there are . . . two! Two ears let us hear "in stereo." Not only does that make music sound better but it also helps us tell the direction the sounds are coming from. We also notice that Rachel's ears are out at just the right angle to pick up sounds the best, and we see that they are shaped sort of like a funnel. All these things are part of God's plan for her to hear as well as possible.

Let's look at Douglas now. In the middle of his face we see two . . . eyes! Yes—and very pretty ones, too. Two eyes are important, also, because they give him depth perception. That means that he can tell how far away things are when he looks at them. God knows that eyes are very delicate, so God has done some things to protect them. Notice that they are set back just a bit and that they are protected by bone. Feel around your own eyes and you will find a ridge of bone surrounding and protecting them. Finally, to help keep them clean, Doug's eyes have what? . . . Yes, lashes and brows, which help catch dust and dirt. And there are eyelids that protect his eyes at night and that can also blink to keep them moist.

Let's look at Amy now. Down here we see her mouth. Notice that the lips are a very special kind of skin. This skin is just right to move for talking or eating. Also, this skin is very sensitive to hot things, so if food is too hot, Amy's lips will tell her before she puts it into her mouth and burns herself.

Finally, let's look at Thomas, and notice what's right in the middle of his face. . . . Yes, it's his nose! . . . Yes, it does stick out a little bit, and that is good, because of the important jobs the nose does. What are those jobs? . . . Yes, the nose breathes in air—and so does the mouth, and it is important that we have two different places where we can get our breath. The nose also smells things, and it can pick up smells by sticking out a little bit. Also, notice where Thomas's nose is located. It is right above his mouth. This is important, because if he is about to take a bite of some food that is spoiled, chances are his nose will smell it before he puts it into his mouth, and he will know not to eat it. That is one more protection that God gives us.

I hope you will think more about some of these things we have discussed today. Maybe you can talk with your family and friends and think of even more ways that God loves us by how our faces are made.

God loves you and made you with such great care! Our faces are made not only to look nice but also to help us be healthy and safe. When you look in a mirror this week, please take time to notice and remember these important things about yourself, and think about how God has made you in such wonderful ways.

36 · A Different Kind of Vision

SCRIPTURE: *Nehemiah 2:2—"Why is your face sad . . . ?*
This is nothing else but sadness of the heart."
OBJECTS: *"Optical illusions" and a ruler.*
CONCEPT: *Our eyes are easily fooled about some things, yet*
they are so amazing in being able to tell what facial
expressions mean.

I want to test you on some things this morning. I have a
book with me that I took out from our local library. It has
some pictures and drawings in it that I want you to look at.
Here is a drawing of two lines on different backgrounds,
and the question that the book wants us to answer is this:
"Which line is longer?"

Can everyone see? Which line do you think is
longer? . . . Yes, Tyler, this red one looks much longer,
doesn't it? But here I have a ruler. Let's measure each
line. . . . Look, they are both exactly four inches! Our eyes
were fooled, weren't they? Though the red line looks longer
than the blue one, they are really both the same.

Let's try another one. . . . We were fooled again,
weren't we? This book is full of these tricks. These tricks
have a special name. Do you know what they are
called? . . . Yes, Tanner, they are called "optical illusions."
That means they play tricks on our eyes. Our eyes really
can be fooled about some things, can't they?

I have a special friend who knows me very well. One day I showed her some of these optical illusions, and do you know what? I fooled her every single time! I teased her and told her that her eyes were not very good at seeing anymore.

The next day I saw this same friend again. For some reason I was feeling very sad on this day, but I didn't want anyone to know. So when I saw my friend, I made a smile and told her I was feeling fine.

But do you know what? She looked at me, and even though I was making a smile, she could tell that I really was sad, and she asked me why. Well, even though I had thought I wanted to hide my feelings, she got me to talk, and I soon felt much better.

If I would hold this ruler up to my face, I wonder if anyone could measure the difference between my smile when I am really happy and my smile when I am really sad but pretending to be happy. It would probably be a very, very tiny difference, wouldn't it? And yet a friend is able to see that difference.

This is something I think is so very special about how God has made us. Our eyes can be tricked about some things, like the lines in "optical illusions." But when we care about someone, it is amazing how much we can see in the lines in his or her face. When we see these things and care about that person, we are able to help as a friend.

Maybe you can get a book of optical illusions and play them with your friends, or maybe your friends sometimes like to play them with you. Whenever you do, I hope you will remember that even though some things may fool us, God has given us eyes to see so clearly when we care about others. I am glad for the ways that all of you are caring persons, and for the things your caring eyes can help you to see and do for one another.

SCRIPTURE: *Psalm 50:1—"God . . . speaks and summons the earth from the rising of the sun to its setting."*
OBJECT: *A night-light.*
CONCEPT: *Our fears are overcome when we are assured that God is with us at all times.*

This *(holds up an object)* is something that comes in many different styles, but I think that no matter what style we see, we can tell what it is. . . . Yes, Thad, this is a night-light. . . . I am glad you and Ben both have one.

Tell me, what is the purpose of a night-light? . . . Ryan? . . . Yes, put it in our bedroom at night, and then we can see a little bit. . . . Very good, Marcie, it helps us not to be afraid of the dark. I think those are all just the right reasons for having a night-light. There is nothing we need to feel silly or bad about if we want to have a small light on in our bedroom. It is a good idea.

One thing about this is a curious thought to me, though. When we are asleep, how are our eyes? . . . Yes, they are closed. When our eyes are closed, falling asleep or being asleep, we cannot see anything, no matter whether there is a light on or not. When we are sleeping, we can't see the light that this night-light is making, and yet it is still very important. The reason it is still very important is that we *know* it is there, and just knowing it is there makes a big difference. We know that if we need to see something, then we are able to, because the night-light keeps shining and shining, all night long.

I want us to think about just one thing about God that is very important. And that is that God is always with us. No matter whether we are playing or going to school or eating or sleeping, God is with us. Believing in God doesn't mean that we are thinking about God's presence every minute, but it does mean that we know that God is always with us, just as we know that our night-light is always shining. And so we go ahead and do the things we need to do and are not afraid. We know that God loves us and is with us and caring for us in every time and every place.

I am glad for night-lights, and for how they shine and shine through every hour of the night. And I am glad for this important lesson that they can help us remember about God—that God is with us always, in every hour of the day or night.

38 · *Bee-lieving We Can!*

SCRIPTURE: *Matthew 17:20—"If you have faith as a grain of mustard seed, . . . nothing will be impossible to you."*
OBJECT: *A picture or other likeness of a bumblebee.*
CONCEPT: *Many things that appear to be impossible are accomplished by people with faith.*

I have here a little magnet that holds things on the refrigerator door at our house. It is shaped like something that you have all seen this summer. . . . Yes, Khammany, it is a bee—and it is a particular kind of bee. It is a bumblebee.

What are some things you can tell me about bumblebees. . . . Yes, Andy, that is true. They do sting. That is the kind of protection that God has given them. But do you know what? A bumblebee will not try to string you unless it thinks you are trying to hurt it. So remember to be very still when you are near a bumblebee, and you will not be stung. What other things are there about bumblebees? . . . Yes, they collect pollen from flowers. . . . Ah, right, Philip, they fly! That is what I want to talk most about today.

Do you know that scientists have studied bumblebees, and the scientists have figured out that the bumblebees should not be able to fly! I guess their bodies are too big compared to their wings, or something like that. Anyway, no one seems to have told the bumblebees about this, because they just keep flying around anyway!

What, Kenneth? . . . Yes, I do remember a couple of weeks ago when a bumblebee came into our church. It just flew and flew, all through the sanctuary, didn't it?

The more I think about bumblebees, the more I think they have much to teach us. Remember, it is supposed to be impossible for them to fly, but they do anyway.

Jesus told us that if we have faith in God, we will be able to do things that might seem impossible otherwise. That is very important to think about.

There are many things that have been done by people that once were thought impossible to do. Once it was thought that no one could run a mile in less than four minutes. But then someone showed that it could be done, and after that many others found they could do it, too. Once it was thought impossible to go to the moon, but people worked together, and we have done that. Doctors have discovered cures for diseases that many people once thought would be impossible to cure.

There are many other examples, too, of things that once were thought to be impossible but have been done by people who believed they could do them.

There may be things that seem so hard for you to learn right now, but you can do it! Believing in the abilities God has given you is the important beginning to your doing them.

As I look around at you, it is very exciting to me to think about all of you and of all the things you will do because of your faith in God and in yourself as you know God is with you.

Remember our friend, the bumblebee. When you see one, think about how it is supposed to be impossible for it to fly—but it flies anyway. And then think about all the things you can do and will do because of how God is with you.

39 · Many Kinds of Growing

SCRIPTURE: *Romans 1:20—"Ever since the creation of the world [God's] invisible nature . . . has been clearly perceived in the things that have been made."*
OBJECT: *Something that is clearly old-fashioned.*
CONCEPT: *God blesses us with the kinds of inventions that help people more and more as time goes on.*

One of my favorite things to learn about is inventors and their inventions. Do any of you like to study inventors? Who are some of the inventors you know, and what things did they invent? . . . Henry Ford . . . George Washington Carver . . . Thomas Edison . . . Madame Curie . . . Very good! You have learned many things. Do any of you think you may be inventors someday? . . . What would you like to invent? . . .

Wow! You have some great ideas!

I have something here that may look strange to you.

Do you know what this is? . . . Yes, Kelly, it is a glove—but a special kind of glove. This is a baseball glove—one that is very old. It was used by Mr. Emch of our church when he played professional baseball more than fifty years ago. Look how small, how different this is from the gloves you are used to seeing now. I'll bet that the gloves you children use now are bigger and better than this one that was once used in a professional league.

This old-fashioned baseball glove is a good example of how things change. People keep wanting to make improvements on what we already have. And so new ideas come about, and new inventions are made. Better things keep coming to us.

Tell me, who gave us our minds to think of new ideas or new inventions? . . . Yes, Jody, God has given us minds that can do this. God makes us be curious and makes us want to try new possibilities, and that is what helps new inventions to come about.

I look around at you, and I can see how you are all growing. You are getting taller and growing on the outside, but you are also each growing in your thinking and feeling on the inside.

There is another kind of growing, too. God is with us as we grow *together*, by working together and learning together. We do this as we find new ideas or inventions that will help each other. Inventors cannot work alone. They use the ideas of other inventors who did things before them. They try to make one more improvement on what someone else did earlier, and so things keep changing a little bit more and a little bit more, even as this baseball glove kept having little improvements made on it, until it finally changed all the way to what we have today.

God has given us such a wonderful world. And God has given us minds to be curious and to want to do better than before. I hope you will notice all the inventions there are that help people. And I hope you will remember that all these things are possible because of how God loves us and is with us as we try to love and help others.

40 · *Always in Style*

SCRIPTURE: *1 Peter 2:9—"But you are a chosen race, a royal priesthood, a holy nation, God's own people."*
OBJECT: *A new-looking pair of blue jeans, but with the designer label missing.*
CONCEPT: *It is who we are and how God has made us that gives us our worth.*

I have a real problem, and I am hoping you can help me figure out what to do about it.

Look, here is a pair of my best blue jeans. You can see that they are in nice condition, and I should be able to wear them many more times. But I'm afraid I can't wear them anymore. Here is the reason. Just look at what has happened. The fancy label on the back pocket of these jeans has come off! You can see right here where it used to be, can't you?

Well, I am very sad, because I know I can't wear these anymore. After all, I want everyone to know that I wear one of the fancy kinds of jeans with a designer label—one of the kinds we see advertised on television. I certainly couldn't be seen wearing a pair of jeans that didn't have one of those labels.

Well, my problem now is to figure out what I should do with these pants. Can you help me with this problem? Should I make them into rags or give them away or what? . . . What, Shawn? You say that I could still wear these jeans, even without a label? How can I do that? Oh, just put them on? Hmmm . . .

Are you telling me that it isn't the most important thing in the world to have designer things, or even new things all the time? . . . Yes, Sheila, that would be a good lesson for me to learn, wouldn't it? Then I could enjoy wearing these pants more times, and I could enjoy many other things more, too.

Many times we see things advertised on television, or hear that many of our friends are getting a certain kind of new toy, and we want that, too. We want to be like everyone else, and have things that are popular. Sometimes it may happen that we do get to have that popular new toy or that brand of clothing that others have, and that is good. But sometimes we will not get to have it, and that is OK, too.

It is OK because what makes us really special is not what we have or what we wear or where we go. What makes us special is how we are made and who we are. God loves us and has made every one of us in a special and loving way. I am just as special, whether my jeans have their label on them anymore or not.

So you are right. I can keep wearing these jeans, and I will. And I hope I will remember, and you will remember, too, what we talked about today. It isn't what we wear or have on the outside that makes us special. It is who we are and how God has made us that gives us our worth.

41 · Avoiding Accidents

SCRIPTURE: *Jeremiah 7:24—". . . and went backward and not forward."*
OBJECT: *A hand-held mirror.*
CONCEPT: *We learn from the past, but even more than this, we know how God is with us as we go forward.*

I have a special kind of mirror here *(holds up a mirror)*. It is from my bicycle. Do you know what kind of mirror this is? . . . Yes, T.J., it is a rear-view mirror. What is a rear-view mirror good for, Jenny? That is right. It helps us to see and know what is behind us.

Do any of you have a mirror like this on your bicycles? . . . A few of you do. They can help us ride safely, because they help us know whether something is coming up from behind us.

Do you know that your family's car has mirrors like this for the driver to see behind the car? . . . Yes, there is always one inside the car and at least one or two on the outside for safer driving.

Well, I have been thinking that if this is good for safer bicycle riding or safer car driving, then it must be good for safer walking, too. So, starting right now, I think I will

---

carry this mirror in my hand and always be watching behind me when I walk. *(Here the leader holds up the mirror and walks around bumping into objects or people because of looking only in the mirror. It is up to each leader to determine to what extent he or she wishes to act this out.)* Yes, there is the pulpit behind me, and . . . oops! Excuse, me, Katie, I didn't see you there. And behind me now is . . . oh! I'm sorry, Jackie. I didn't mean to step on your foot . . . and I'm sorry about bumping you, Michelle.

Don't you think that carrying this mirror is going to help me be safer as I walk about? . . . What? You don't think so? . . . Why don't you think it will help me be safer, Jonathan? . . . I think I see what you mean. I am so busy looking behind me that I am not paying enough attention to what is in front of me, am I?

A rear-view mirror is very good for safety, but only if we look in it a *little bit* every now and then. If you watch your mom or dad when they are driving, you will notice that they look in the mirror just for a second or two, every now and then. That is the safest way.

It is very important to think about where we have already been and what we have already done, and to learn from the things we have already done. We know that God has been with us in every thing that has ever happened in our lives—in all the things that are behind us in our living.

But it is even more important to be paying attention to where we are right now and to where we are going right now. As much as all the things of the past are important and have been good, we know that the future—because of God's love—can be even better.

Wonderful things have happened in our church in the past. With God's guidance, even better things will be ahead. Wonderful things have already happened in the life of each one of you. But because of God's love, even better things will be ahead.

I don't think I will keep on carrying this rear-view mirror. You think that is a good decision? . . . Fine. It is important to be paying attention and thinking about what is behind us and has already happened. But most of our attention needs to be on what is ahead of us and on how God will be with us wherever we go, making the future even better.

---

42 · *Not Like Everyone Else*

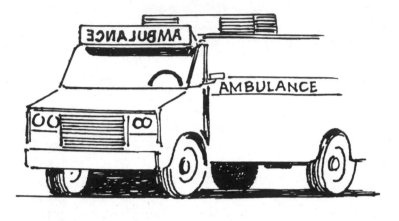

SCRIPTURE: *1 Corinthians 12:4—"Now there are varieties of gifts, but the same Spirit."*
OBJECTS: *Letters printed backward, on poster board and a stand on which to place them.*
CONCEPT: *Being different from the rest can be very good and very important.*

The other day I saw something that was really silly. Someone had painted some letters to make a sign, and the person must not have learned the alphabet very well, because the letters were all written backward! Can you imagine that?

For example, here is the way the letter B looked on the sign. And here is how the other letters were made—an L, a C, an N, and a U and an E.

When I saw these letters all mixed together, I just couldn't believe it. Someone had made a bad mistake, I thought. There could never be any reason for all these mistakes, I decided.

Not only was each letter backwards, but the whole word didn't sound like one I had ever heard before. It said "ecnalubma" which is a very strange word, isn't it? But do you know what? It turned out that all of this wasn't a mistake after all. Do you know why all of these letters were put together in this way? What, Jeremy? You've seen something like this on an emergency vehicle? You're getting way ahead of me, aren't you?

Yes, if we add two A's and an M—which are the same backward or forward—and put them in the order that I saw them, this is how they look. . . . Yes, Cassie, it says "ambulance," but it says it backward. And why is it backward? . . . Very good, Sherry. It is for when the ambulance comes up behind other cars.

When a driver looks in her mirror to see what is behind her, the mirror makes everything look backward. So, when these letters, written backward and placed in reverse order, are seen in the mirror, they will turn around to be the right way! The driver will know immediately that an ambulance is behind her and may be rushing to an accident or taking someone to a hospital. So these letters are not so silly after all. They help to save lives because they help other drivers to know very quickly that an ambulance, which may be in a great hurry, is behind them.

Do you know what? I can remember times in my life when I have seen another person who was different in some way, and I thought it was something pretty silly. I also can remember times when there was something different about me, and I felt bad about it, because I wanted to be exactly like everyone else.

But do you know something else? I have learned that no one is exactly like anyone else. God has made all of us different. We look different. We like different colors or foods. We can each do different things well. God has made each one of us to be very special in our own way. Because of this, we each have special things we are able to offer others.

I hope you will notice the next time you see an emergency vehicle with backward letters on it, and think about how important it is that those letters *are* backward. And remember how other people who are different from you are special in their own ways, and how God has made you different and special in your own ways, too.

---

43 · No Help Needed!

SCRIPTURE: *Isaiah 65:18—"But be glad and rejoice for ever in that which I create."*

OBJECTS: *A small branch with fall leaves and a bottle of glue.*

CONCEPT: *God's plan is wondrous, and so complete, as seen in the world of nature.*

I am really worried about something. This is a problem that seems very serious—and I am going to ask for your help in doing something about it.

Look what I have here! Just look at this branch! And this is only one small part of many like it that I have been noticing lately. All over our town, I see leaves dying on trees, and I am worried about those trees that must be dying, too, since their leaves are falling off.

Well, I have a plan, but I need your help. Are some of you good tree climbers? . . . Yes? Nevin is . . . and Caleb . . . and others, too? Great, because we will need some good tree climbers. With my plan, some of us are going to have to get way up high in the trees, while others of us can reach the low branches.

Here is my plan. We will get a bottle of glue for each one of us, and we will go all over town and help every tree that is losing its leaves. Look . . . with a little bit of glue, I think we can help each leaf to hold on, and then the trees can all get better.

What do you think of my plan? Are you ready to get started this afternoon? You'd better wear old clothes. How many of you can get started helping me this afternoon? . . . What? It looks like only a couple of you are interested. . . . What, Melinda? You think it would be a pretty silly thing to do? Why do you say that? . . . Can what Melinda just said be true? Do the trees really want to have their leaves fall off like this, Shawn? You all seem to agree—and you are right. We don't need to help these trees, do we? This is all part of God's plan. The trees are doing just what they are supposed to do!

Every year the trees of our area go through a cycle. They grow all new leaves in the spring, and in the fall they lose their leaves when they start to get ready for winter. It is all a part of God's plan, isn't it? This is the way these trees stay healthy and keep growing.

We can watch the changes in the trees, and we can be glad and enjoy all the changes. But we don't have to worry, and we don't have to try to help with glue or anything else. This is all happening just according to God's plan.

As we watch the leaves change and enjoy the changes, let's remember how wonderful God's world is. And let's remember that the same God who figured out such a marvelous way to take care of the trees all year around also is taking care of each one of us all year around.

44 · Walking with Awareness

SCRIPTURE: *1 Corinthians 12:21—"The eye cannot say to the hand, 'I have no need of you,' nor again the head to the feet, 'I have no need of you.'"*

OBJECT: *A good pair of walking shoes.*

CONCEPT: *Our feet are often taken for granted, but they are such an important gift from God and are given great importance in the Bible.*

Recently I read how many steps the average person takes in just one day. Do you have any guess about what that number might be? How many steps do you think people take in an average day, just walking around the house or walking to school or in a store? . . . Mae says one hundred . . . Anna thinks two thousand . . . What, Adam? . . . a million! Maybe you do take that many steps sometimes! The number that I read was seven thousand. The average person takes seven thousand steps just doing regular things each day.

Now I know that many of you, with all the running and playing you do, probably take far more than that on most days. But that is quite a number, isn't it? That is about two miles of walking each day, without even *trying* to walk far.

This afternoon many of us are going to be walking, on purpose, much farther than that, because we are going to be walking ten miles to raise money for hungry people. . . . Yes, Mae, your family did make a pledge—and so did many others in our church.

There is something about walking that is extra important. Not only do we go so many miles and keep track of the miles for our sponsors to give the money they've promised, but the walking itself is important. Walking seems to make us think about things more. Walking makes us more aware of things. Sometimes people who need to make an important decision about something will go for a walk to think about it. . . . Do you know people like that? . . . Yes, the walking itself helps us think and makes the deciding a little easier.

Today, as we walk, every step we take will help us think more about people who are hungry and about how we can do more in our lives to help them or to help others who are in need.

With every step we take, what do we use? What is hitting the ground, or hitting the street, every time? . . . Of course—our feet! That is why I have brought these shoes with me to show to you this morning. These are the ones I will be wearing this afternoon, and they are especially good for walking. You can see that they give extra-good support and protection for my feet.

Sometimes we take our feet for granted. But they are important, and we need to take care of them so they can keep doing all the things they do for us. We need to keep our shoes on properly, walk correctly, and do all we can to take good care of our feet so they can take good care of us!

In the Bible, feet are given much importance. People then did not have cars or airplanes. They had to walk most of the places they wanted to go. There are many Bible verses that talk about feet and how important they are. Jesus even washed the feet of his disciples as a way of caring for them. In the new *Book of Worship* of our church, there is a service for foot washing, based on what Jesus did for his disciples.

Those of us who are able to walk are so blessed. That is such a gift, and we need to be aware of how blessed we are to be able to walk. Those of us with enough food to eat are so blessed, too. That is also a gift, and we need to be aware of how blessed we are in that way.

I am glad for walks that help us to become more aware and that help us to do good thinking and make good decisions. I am glad for our walk this afternoon that has made us more aware of those who are hungry. I am glad that our walking today will be a help for those in need.

I hope you are also glad for God's gift of feet. Let's take good care of our feet, and always remember how blessed we are in all the walking that we do every day.

(Note: In using this sermon, the leader must be especially sensitive to the fact that some people are unable to walk. Within the congregation or perhaps within the group of children themselves, there may be someone who needs assistance in walking or who uses a wheelchair. The leader needs to approach the topic with the idea of how blessed are those who can walk, but also that the ability to walk does not show greater favor from God than that given to persons unable to walk. Those who cannot walk are blessed to give and share in other special ways.)

45 · The One Not Handicapped

SCRIPTURE: *Proverbs 11:3—"The integrity of the upright guides them."*

OBJECTS: *Objects associated with physical handicaps may be used but are not necessary.*

CONCEPT: Every person is handicapped in some ways and very capable in others. What is inside us is more important than the outside in terms of much that we can do or be.

This morning I want to talk with you about something that is a serious subject. I want to talk with you about conditions sometimes called handicaps. Do you know what a handicap is? . . . That is a good answer, Ryan. It is a limitation of some sort. What are some examples of handicaps that you know? . . . Yes, blindness, or being deaf . . .

or not having the full use of one's arms or legs . . . these are all types of handicaps. These examples that you have named are the ones we tend to notice most easily because the condition requires the use of a chair or special cane or other items that catch our attention.

The first handicapping condition you mentioned was blindness, and I want to tell you a story about a person who was blind.

When I was a student, the college I attended had a fire in one of its dormitories. A dormitory is a building in which the students live. It is their home at college while they are away from their own homes. The fire started in the middle of the night, and it spread very quickly. Because it was night, it was dark outside and the students were all asleep inside the building. Then, the lights in the building all went out because the fire made the power go off.

One of the students who lived in this dormitory, was blind. His name was Gerald. Gerald could do many things all alone and could take care of himself in most ways, but I remember that he often had to have help in going from place to place during the school day.

Well, when the fire started and was spreading in some parts of the dormitory, it was still very dark in most all the places where the fire had not yet reached. People were very frightened because they could not see. Many of them panicked. That means they were so frightened they did not know what to do, because it was dark and they could not see where to go.

That was when Gerald who was blind made the difference. Because he could not see, he had learned so much more about their building. He knew how many steps there were on each staircase. He knew how many steps it would take to get from any one place to another in the halls. He knew when to be ready for curves or tricky places. And because Gerald knew so much that others did not know, he was able to stay calm, and he was able to lead many of the students safely out of the building. As a matter of fact, everyone was able to get out of the building even though the whole dormitory burned down. This young man made much of the difference in helping this to be true.

Some handicapping conditions are easy to notice. Those are the ones that we mentioned right away when we named some handicaps. But there are many other kinds of handicaps, too—ones that we don't usually think about. It is a handicap for us that we do not notice things the way Gerald noticed them. We do not learn how far things are, how many steps there are, how things feel to touch, and so many more things like that.

In the dark, because he *had* noticed these things, Gerald was the only one who was *not* handicapped. Everyone else was handicapped in that situation.

What I hope you will remember from this story is that we can never say that one person definitely is handicapped and another definitely is not. Everyone is handicapped in some ways, and not in other ways.

What makes the important difference is what we feel inside us. It was the special feeling of being able to care and to help that made other students want to help Gerald whenever he needed assistance in his day-to-day activities. And it was the same inner feeling of wanting to care and help that made Gerald do what he did for others in different times—especially during the fire.

Remember, it is what is inside you, much more than what is outside, that makes you be who you are and that makes you able to care and to do the things you can do.

46 · God's Got the Whole World

SCRIPTURE: *Genesis 1:1—"In the beginning God created the heavens and the earth."*
OBJECT: *A globe.*
CONCEPT: *God created the whole world, and all people are part of that one world.*

This weekend we are celebrating a holiday. Yes, most of you will get the day off from school tomorrow because of this holiday. Do you know what this day is called? . . . Right, Victor, it is Columbus Day. Who was Columbus, anyway, and why do we have a day in honor of him? . . .

That's excellent, Derek. All those things are true. Christopher Columbus discovered America in 1492. Some of you even have learned that poem, haven't you? "In fourteen hundred and ninety-two, Columbus sailed the ocean blue."

There was something very important that Columbus believed, something that made him brave enough to make his trip on the ocean and helped him discover our land. What was that? . . . That is right, Heath. He believed the world was round. Almost everybody else in his time believed that the earth was flat and that they would fall off the edge if they sailed too far. So Columbus had a very different and very great idea.

Here is a globe of what we now know our world looks like. This helps us see that our world is round, just as Columbus thought. Look, here is the place where Christopher Columbus started his voyage . . . and he sailed in this direction . . . and he landed . . . here!

Where did Columbus think he was when he landed here? . . . Yes, Ian, he thought he had gone all the way to India. That is why he called the people here "indians." Actually, they were native people of these lands, and it would be better to call them "native Americans" or to call them by the names of their tribes.

Let's look at the globe and notice a few other things. Right now it is daylight time where we live—in the western Hemisphere. But over here in the eastern Hemisphere, what is happening? . . . Yes, it is dark, or getting dark. Right now it is fall here in the northern hemisphere where we live. What is happening in the southern hemisphere? . . . Yes, it is springtime now, and they will soon have summer while we are having winter.

The whole world is round. The whole world is connected. God made us so that we all can learn about one another. God made us so all people in the world have nighttime and daytime. God made us so that even people who live far apart from one another have many things in common.

We know that God made the whole, big, round world. The whole world is full of beautiful places, and the whole world really is in God's hands. How glad we are that we know this—not only on Columbus Day but every day!

47 · Trying to Catch the Wind

SCRIPTURE: *Job 38:24—"What is the way to the place where the light is distributed, or where the east wind is scattered upon the earth?"*

OBJECTS: *Autumn leaves.*

CONCEPT: *Some activities can help us feel more a part of God's creation.*

This is one of my favorite times of the year. Do you like the autumn, too? . . . Good. Tell me what some of the things are that you like to do in this time of the year. . . . Those are all good, fun things!

There is another name for this season, and it is . . . fall. That's right. Why do you think this season has come to have that name? . . . Yes, Amanda, it is because the leaves are falling from the trees during this time of the year. Some of the things you told me you like about this season have to do with the leaves. I want to tell you something that I like so much, and it is a fun game with the leaves.

What I like to do is to catch leaves that are falling from a tree. I try to catch them before they touch the ground. The way that this is most fun of all for me is to stand under a very tall tree where there is room all around to run and be safe. The best place to go is to the park, or to a big backyard, where there are no cars nearby.

On a day like this, when the leaves are falling from the tree, I stand under the tree and watch as a leaf from way up high comes loose and starts to fall. I watch it and watch it, and as the wind blows it, I have to keep running at just the same speed as the wind is blowing, so I can stay right under it until it gets close to the ground. Then, as it is still swirling and moving, just before it touches the ground, I try to catch it.

Do you think that this sounds fun? . . . Yes? Most of you do.

Have you tried to do this, Melissa? This is something I enjoy so much because it helps me think about all the ways the wind blows. It speeds up and slows down. It swirls. It is so amazing! Here . . . just by trying to catch a leaf when I drop it toward you . . . you can see how tricky this can be! Well, it is much more tricky and much more fun outside in the wind, when the leaf has started to fall from way up high.

Playing this game helps me think even more about how wonderful God's world is. So many things that happen every day are important. The sun shines. The wind blows. The clouds form and sometimes make rain. Every day, all these things and more are happening. Sometimes I notice them and say "thank you" to God, but many times I don't think at all about how wonderful all these things are.

In different parts of the Bible we are reminded of how great God's creation is. I am glad for these words. I am also glad for things we can do to help us know and feel the greatness of God's creation.

I hope you will try this game we have discussed. I hope you will try to catch leaves by running with the wind and noticing the wind as you do so. I hope you will be aware, more and more, of the wonders of God's world.

---

48 · For the Birds?—No, for Us!

SCRIPTURE: *Ephesians 2:19—"So then you are no longer strangers and sojourners, but you are fellow citizens with the saints and members of the household of God."*
OBJECTS: *The children themselves.*
CONCEPT: *There is much we can learn from Canadian geese that will be good for us and for our church.*

Lately, I have been seeing something happening over and over in the sky. I have been seeing birds that have been starting to fly in a certain direction. Do you know what direction that would be? . . . Right, Garry, they are flying south, to where it will be warm for the winter. What, Dawn? . . . Yes, your grandpa does fly south for the winter, too, doesn't he? But he needs an airplane to make his trip!

There is one kind of bird I especially like to watch when they fly south. I like most of all to watch Canadian geese. When they fly together they always make the shape of a letter. Let's see . . . is it a letter B or a Q that they make? . . . Oh, yes, it is a letter V, isn't it? Thank you, Kevin.

I have been learning some very interesting things about Canadian geese lately, and I want us to pretend that we are geese while we talk about them. Everyone who wants to be a Canadian goose this morning, please stand here in this line. . . . OK, let's get into our V . . . and let's start to flap those wings! *(Here the leader may take a minute or two to get the children arranged into a V shape, and then continue to move or direct them in the further actions referred to in the sermon.)*

The first thing I have learned about these geese is that by making a V and staying together in this formation, they can go much farther. Each bird's wings are making wind that helps to pull along the goose right behind it, This means that the goose who is at the front has to work the hardest and really flap while up there. Amy, since you are at the lead right now, you need to be flapping extra hard. I have learned that the geese can go about one and one-half times farther in a day of flying this way then they could if they were all flying alone, because of the advantages of working together.

The goose who is in the lead gets tired after a little while, so she then drops back in the line where she can work less hard and rest a little. . . . Now Brian is in the lead—so you must flap the hardest!

I have also learned that Canadian geese care about one another. If one gets hurt, others help. Let us suppose that Lisa has hurt her wing and cannot fly. The geese will all land and wait to see whether she can get better. If it will take a while for her to heal, then three or four other geese will wait with her, getting food and protecting her, until she is able to fly. Then they can make their own little V and begin on their way again together.

Hey! Some of us aren't flapping very hard! Let's keep going—and, Brian, why don't you move down now and let Andy lead for a while? . . .

There are many things we can learn from Canadian geese—about how we get along at church or at home or at school. Let's remember how much better it is for everyone when we work together. Let's also remember to take turns being leaders, because that is good for everyone, too. Remember, also, how the geese care about one another when one is hurt or cannot keep up, and how good it is for all of us when we do that, too.

Our church is a very caring place. By remembering all the things we have learned about Canadian geese, we can help it be an even happier place.

---

49 · Thirsty for More

SCRIPTURE: *John 4:14—"Whoever drinks . . . will never thirst."*

OBJECTS: *Enough plastic, disposable communion cups for each child to have one.*

CONCEPT: *The meaning of communion is partly the quenching of a thirst that is more than physical.*

Our congregation is taking part with Christian churches all through the world this morning in having communion, as this is Worldwide Communion Sunday. You can see the plates and cups that are on our altar for the communion service that will soon begin.

I have told you that we would talk more about what communion means and about some of the reasons it is such an important time for the members of our church. Let's talk a little bit more about that right now.

You can see that there are plates and a cup up here. These are similar to the things that we would put on the table at home if we were helping to set the table for a meal, aren't they? Why would there be things up here that would look like items for a meal? . . . Yes, Jamie, it is because we are remembering the meal of Jesus with the disciples—the meal we call the Lord's Supper.

At a meal we have something to eat and something to drink. The same is true of the communion meal, so it is very similar—but it is very different, too.

I want you to imagine with me that you have just been outside on a hot day, and you have been running and playing hard for a long time. Now you have come in for a drink. Tell me, would you want a little drink or a big drink now? . . . Holly says a big drink! I think all of us would want that, wouldn't we?

Look at what I have here. This is a cup just like the ones we use in our communion services. If you tried to get a drink from this cup, do you think it would be enough? . . . No, Tracy, I don't think so, either. But this is what we use for our drink in communion. It isn't a kind of cup to drink from so we won't be thirsty in the regular way, but it is for a different kind of thirst that is deep inside us. When we understand what Jesus did for us, then drinking from this cup helps us not to be thirsty in that deep inside way anymore.

That's a hard thing to try to understand, but I hope you will think about that some more. I am going to give one of these cups to each one of you to take home. I hope you will get a drink of water with this cup today, and see that it is not very big at all and doesn't give you very much to drink. Then I hope you will keep this cup—maybe in your room— and think more about this. Think about how much Jesus loved us and loves us still. Think about how Jesus satisfied the thirst deep inside of us.

An important part of communion is this understanding—and how we feel when we know the love God has for us through the great gift of Jesus.

50 · And the Winner Is . . .

SCRIPTURE: *Romans 8:16—"We are children of God."*
OBJECT: *A small mirror, preferably in a frame.*
CONCEPT: *Each of us is God's child, most loved by God.*

Just this past week I was given something that can help us learn a big secret. Someone gave something to me, and now I have the secret, and this morning I am going to share it with you. Are you ready? Would you like to learn this secret? . . .

Someone gave me this picture. Right now we can see only the back of it, because of the way I am holding it against me *(hold mirror in picture frame)*, but on the other side, I have learned, is a picture of the person in all the world that God loves most of all. Can any of you keep the secret if you look at it? I hope so.

What, Leah? You think this will be a picture of Jesus? That is a good thought. In many ways we can say that Jesus is the person God loves most. I wonder whose picture is here. . . .

Shelly, I am going to let you come over to look at the picture, but don't tell anybody who it is. *(Here the leader acts very secretive, taking one child aside to let only her see into the other side of the picture—which is actually a mirror.)* OK? . . . there . . . shhh . . . ! Don't tell!

Jason, how about you? There . . . don't tell anyone. Others of you who can keep a secret may peek, too. . . .

Wait a minute! Why are the ones who saw the picture smiling and giggling so much? And what's all this whispering to each other about? . . . What, Jory? It's a mirror? What do you . . . let me look. . . . Why, it *is* a mirror! How could that be? What kind of picture is that?

Yes, Saul, that is right. Whoever looks into it sees a picture of himself or herself. Every person is God's favorite person. Each one of you is the person in the whole world that God loves the most. And that is why Jesus came to us—to show that God loves each and every one of us so, so much.

There is one thing I said this morning that turns out not to be true. I thought this was a secret. But it isn't a secret, is it? We know that God loves every person the most, that every person is God's special child. We know that because of Jesus and because of all the teachings in the Bible. It isn't a secret, after all, and we can tell everyone this happy news. As we are observing Thanksgiving this week, and giving thanks for all our blessings, let's remember to give thanks for the greatest blessing of all. Let's give thanks for God's love that is for each and every one of us, thanks for the love that makes every one of us the most special and loved child of God.

A mirror is a good reminder for us of this happy news. Whenever you see yourself in a mirror, I hope you will think of how special you are to God. Sometimes you will see yourself looking happy, and other times looking sad. Sometimes you will notice ways that you are growing or changing, and that's special, too. But no matter how you are, God loves you—you, Jessica, and you, Rebecca—and each one of you, so, so much, just the way you are right now.

51 · *Individual and Together*

SCRIPTURE: *1 Corinthians 1:10—". . . that you be united in the same mind and the same judgment."*
OBJECTS: *A few fall-colored leaves.*
CONCEPT: *God has made each of us in a unique way, yet we can join together to accomplish much good.*

This is one of my favorite times of the year, because the falling leaves make it so pretty outside. I have some leaves here that I think are especially pretty. Do you ever pick up and save leaves that you think are the prettiest? . . . Good!

How many leaves do you think are out there right now? Just in our town, how many do you think there are? . . . Eightyseven? . . . Yes, I'd say at least that many! Sara says "hundreds" . . . now I hear "thousands." . . . Yes, there probably are millions of them, just in our city.

Out of all those leaves, don't you think there must be at least two that are *exactly* the same? . . . You are right,

Lucy. Many are similar, but no two are exactly the same. God has made each one a little bit different. When you find two that you think are the same, look at them closely and you will find that there are some differences between them. God's power of creation is really amazing, isn't it? And the same is true about you—only even more so. Every person is different from all others. Even twins, like Benji and Freddy or Amy and Lisa, are very different. They like different things and can do different things, and even though they look so much alike, there still are differences in who they are! Everyone is special in God's world!

What is your favorite thing to do with leaves in the fall? . . . That is mine, too! They are fun to jump on, when we pile them up high, aren't they? What if I put these three leaves that I have brought here this morning in a nice pile? Do they look as though they would make a nice place for us to jump on? . . . No, it would hurt if we landed on this pile, wouldn't it? We need a big pile for jumping.

Every leaf is different from every other one in the whole world. Yet all the leaves come together to make a beautiful world for us to see. And whole bunches of leaves can be joined together for us to have fun playing.

People are all different, and all very special too. Yet we can all join together to do things we could not do alone or even in groups of two or three. Our church is a good example of this. Even though we have our own ways of looking and thinking—because that is how God has made us—we still join together in worship and in work, and make our city and our world a more beautiful place.

Our church also joins together with other churches in some ways. Our Neighbors in Need offering is a good example of this. People of our church and thousands of other churches are all putting their offerings together to do some very important things to help persons of our nation who are in need right now.

When you see pretty leaves on the trees, or are playing in them, I hope you will remember what we have talked about this morning and will think about how we are all different. Yet we all work together, as Christians, to accomplish many important things.

52 · It All Depends

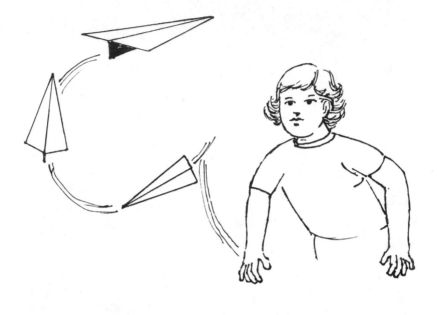

SCRIPTURE: *Matthew 22:17—"Is it lawful to pay taxes to Caesar, or not?"*

OBJECT: *A paper airplane.*

CONCEPT: *Things are not good or evil in themselves but in how we use them.*

Can you tell what I am doing with this piece of paper? Can you tell what I am making from it? *(Here the leader takes time to fold the paper into the shape of an airplane. It may be very simple or quite elaborate, depending on the leader's own variation.)* Yes, it is pretty easy to see that I am making . . . yes . . . almost . . . a paper airplane. There are many different ways to make a paper airplane. This style is my favorite one.

I want to ask you a question. Tell me, is a paper airplane a good thing or a bad thing? Help me to think about this, will you? What are some things that might make us think a paper airplane is bad? . . . Freddy? . . . Yes, it is bad if a person makes one while he should be listening to the teacher in class, or it is bad if she throws it during school or during any time when it would bother other people. . . . Yes, a paper airplane could also be bad if it is thrown hard at somebody, especially near somebody's face.

OK, what about good things? What might make us think a paper airplane is good? . . . Great, Benji! Yes, it is a *fun* thing to make and to play with, isn't it? It is fun to try making different styles, and certainly fun to watch them fly. . . . Yes, those are other good things. It can teach us about air currents, and it can help us to meet new friends.

Well, now I'm more confused than before. I can't decide if this is a good thing or a bad thing. . . . What, Justin? . . . Yes, I think you are right. It all depends on how we use it. *We* decide if a paper airplane is going to be a good thing or a bad thing.

God gives us so many things, and almost all of them can be for good or for bad, depending on how we use them. God has given us all the earth and told us that we are *stewards* of it. That means it is ours to take care of and to use in the ways that will bring out the most good.

I want to tell you about an inventor. Many years ago there lived a man whose name was Alfred Nobel. One of the things he invented was dynamite. Late in his life he happened to read a story about his invention in the newspaper. The writer of the article talked about how Nobel's invention could be used to make more wars by making bigger bombs and hurting more people. This story made Alfred Nobel very sad. He had invented dynamite because he knew it could be used for good things. It could break up huge rocks and help dig tunnels or mine things from deep in the ground. This had been his hope for his invention.

Alfred Nobel made much money as a result of his invention, so he took a large part of it and established a special fund. Money from that fund is awarded each year to encourage people who are working to better the lives of all people. These awards are called the Nobel prize. . . . Very good, Brenda. Martin Luther King, Jr., is one of the persons who has been awarded the Nobel prize for peace.

Alfred Nobel did this because he wanted everyone always to know he did not want his invention to be used for war but for helpful things in the best interests of humanity.

I hope you will remember the story of Alfred Nobel. I hope you will pay attention if you hear a story in the news sometime about the Nobel prize. Dynamite could be used for very good things or for very bad things. Nobel wanted people to choose to do good things.

I also hope you will think of some of these things whenever you make a paper airplane. You must decide if you will use it for good things or for bad. That is how God has made us and our world. God does not make things be good or bad, but lets us choose how to use all that we have and can do.

Let's try to find the good in what God gives us, because we are stewards, caring for God's world. And let's be like Alfred Nobel and try to get other people to see the good, and work together to care for one another, living together in peace.

Concluding Thought

EVERY TIME I READ the closing chapter of A. A. Milne's *The House at Pooh Corner*, my eyes fill with tears. Christopher Robin tells his Pooh Bear that he will no longer be seeing him as much. It is hard to explain why, but it has something to do with "Factors" (A. A. Milne, *The House at Pooh Corner* [New York: E.P. Dutton & Co., 1928 and 1956], p. 177).

There is reason for the tears in the eyes. Yet there is even more reason for a smile on the lips and contentment in the heart. This is part of how growing together in wisdom and in stature takes its form.

For every child, there comes that time of deciding that he or she is now "too old" to come forward for a children's sermon. For each child, the age at which this occurs will be different—and in each case there is reason for sadness. But there is even more reason for smiling contentment. In a very real way, this marks a rite of passage in the young person's life. And though the time of the child's active involvement in the children's sermons as a participant may be past, still the relationship shared—and, yes, even some of the lessons—will continue as a part of that young person in all ways as time goes on.

A very special joy for me has occurred on a number of occasions when one of these "children's sermon graduates" has come to me with ideas that perhaps I might sometime use for a children's sermon. Such a child is a "graduate," indeed, for he or she has truly learned to see the world through the eyes of faith that God is always with them, and that there are lessons of God's love to be seen in so many of the things they are continuing to do.

Still greater rewards of children's sermons may lie in years yet to come, as these children become teenagers and then adults, and as their growing continues in all ways to be influenced by the ways that they experienced positively the love of God as a very special and accepted member of God's worshiping family.

Index of Scriptures